WITH SPECIAL THANKS TO
NINJA THEORY

D0889469

Others

Edited by Charles Fernyhough

BY THE SAME AUTHOR

The Auctioneer
The Baby in the Mirror
Pieces of Light
A Box of Birds
The Voices Within

OTHERS

*Writers on the power of words to help us see
beyond ourselves*

Edited by Charles Fernyhough

unbound

First published in 2019

Unbound

6th Floor Mutual House, 70 Conduit Street, London W1S 2GF

www.unbound.com

All rights reserved

'Tuesday Lunch' © Leila Aboulela, 2019.
'Stranger', 'abutment' and 'Stars' © Gillian Allnutt, from *wake*, Bloodaxe Books, 2018.
'Look Not with the Eyes' © Damian Barr, 2019.
'A Deep and Persistent Shame' © Noam Chomsky, previously
published online on DiEM25.org, 5 May 2016.
'Is Queueing Politely Really the British Way?' © Rishi Dastidar, 2019.
'Fast as Lightning' © Peter Ho Davies, from *The Fortunes*, Sceptre, 2016.
'Are You Part-Something?' © Louise Doughty, 2019.
'We Are the Champions' © Salena Godden, 2019.
'Sounds of Blackness' © Colin Grant, 2019.
'Bodies' © Sam Guglani, 2019.
'Others ' © Matt Haig, 2019.
'Bridges' © Aamer Hussein, previously published in
37 Bridges and Other Stories, HarperCollins India, 2015.
'In the Dark' © Anjali Joseph, extract from *Keeping in Touch*, 2019.
'Point for Lost Children' © A. L. Kennedy, 2019.
'Excuse Me, but Your Otherness Is Showing' © Joanne Limburg, 2019.
'The Other Side of Gender' © Rachel Mann, 2019.
'Emily Brontë's Bath' © Tiffany Murray, 2019.
'Things Unspoken' © Sara Nović, previously published in
The Massachusetts Review, vol. 55, pp. 298–304, 2014.
'The Leavers of Boston' © Edward Platt, 2019.
'Choosing Sides' © Alex Preston, 2019.
'A Short Story' © Tom Shakespeare, 2019.
'The A–Z of an Earthquake Zone' © Kamila Shamsie, previously published in
Nethra, International Centre for Ethnic Studies, Sri Lanka, May–August 2007.
'Original Sin' © Will Storr, 2019.
'I, Jay' © Preti Taneja, 2019.
'Living in a Country of Words: The Shelter of Stories' © Marina Warner, 2019.
Excerpt from 'Bearer-Beings and Stories in Transit/Storie in Transito', by Marina Warner
in *Marvels & Tales: Journal of Fairy-Tale Studies*, vol. 31, no. 1, pp. 149–162 © 2017 Wayne State
University Press, with the permission of Wayne State University Press.

The rights of Leila Aboulela, Gillian Allnutt, Damian Barr, Noam Chomsky, Rishi Dastidar, Peter
Ho Davies, Louise Doughty, Charles Fernyhough, Selena Godden, Colin Grant, Sam Guglani, Matt
Haig, Aamer Hussein, Anjali Joseph, A. L. Kennedy, Joanne Limburg, Rachel Mann, Tiffany Murray,
Sara Nović, Edward Platt, Alex Preston, Tom Shakespeare, Kamila Shamsie, Will Storr, Preti Taneja,
and Marina Warner to be identified as the authors of this work has been asserted in accordance with
Section 77 of the Copyright, Designs and Patents Act, 1988. No part of this publication may be copied,
reproduced, stored in a retrieval system, or transmitted, in any form or by any means without the prior
permission of the publisher, nor be otherwise circulated in any form of binding or cover other than that
in which it is published and without a similar condition being imposed on the subsequent purchaser.

While every effort has been made to trace the owners of copyright material reproduced
herein, the publisher would like to apologise for any omissions and will be pleased to incorporate
missing acknowledgements in any further editions.

Text Design by PDQ

A CIP record for this book is available from the British Library

ISBN 978-1-78352-751-9 (trade paperback)
ISBN 978-1-78352-752-6 (ebook)
ISBN 978-1-78352-753-3 (limited edition hardback)

Printed in Great Britain by Clays Ltd, Elcograf S.p.A

To the others that we are

Foreword

Richard Holloway

Great novelists don't tell, they *show*. By revealing the complexity of the human condition, they get their readers to understand what makes their characters behave the way they do, even if they don't like the result. It is no surprise that it was a novelist that got the process into two words: *Only connect*. They were used by E. M. Forster as the epigraph to his novel, *Howards End*, about the sexual hypocrisy of Edwardian England. It's about the way people fail to connect their own accidental good fortune with the accidental misfortune of others. But it goes even deeper than that.

There is a doctrine called *predestination*, found in both Christianity and Islam, that makes the same point. It's as if God were a novelist plotting a story. Calvin puts it like this: 'By predestination we mean the eternal decree of God, by which he determined with himself whatever he wished to happen with regard to every man. All are not created on equal terms, but some are preordained to eternal life, others to eternal damnation...'

In our time predestination has been taken over by geneticists who tell us that our future lies not in our stars but in our DNA, and the plot line was written for us long before we were born. Again, it is the writer we must listen to. *Only connect.* Try to understand what makes people act the way they do. Reach back into their story and the factors that determined them. Be dismayed at the result, if you must, but try to understand the forces that formed them.

And understand yourself in the same way. Don't shrink from the truth of what you have become. The past was never under your control. The future might be, but only if you bring them together. If we brought that compassionate realism to the way we judge ourselves and others we might take what Edward St Aubyn calls 'the tramlines of the past' into a new direction in the future.

That, I believe, is what this rich tapestry of a book is trying to get us to achieve. Only connect…

Contents

A TARDIS OF SOULS

Introduction

Charles Fernyhough

Something extraordinary happens around a quarter of the way through Colson Whitehead's 2016 Pulitzer Prize-winning novel, *The Underground Railroad*. We are on a cotton plantation in antebellum Georgia, following the struggles of the slave girl Cora to maintain some semblance of human dignity in the face of an inconceivably brutal regime. Inconceivable, and yet the author gives us the tools to imagine it. We are taken into Cora's world as she works and fights, is raped and cheated and beaten. We are agonised by a brutality that seems to defy the logic of any human heart or brain. Cora and her fellows are not just people reduced to chattels; they are objects of a violence designed to assuage an empty soul, to beat out an identity by negating someone else's. We look out on the world that Cora sees: the brittle pleasures of an old slave's birthday celebrations; the plotting of what seems like an impossible, suicidal escape; the chasing of the mundane joys that remind her of what seems a risible truth: that she is still a human being.

And then the author does this thing. All of a sudden, with nothing more than a chapter break and the signpost of the title

1

'Ridgeway', we are in someone else's point of view. Ridgeway, the six-and-a-half-foot-tall son of a blacksmith, who seeks an alternative to the limited destiny available to him and finds it in rounding up runaway slaves. To make up for his own lack of purpose, he drags absconders back to plantations for certain torture and likely death. We don't just get an objective account of the making of a monster; we see it from the monster's perspective. We learn what it feels like to thrill to the pursuit of a defenceless slave: the cuts and bruises in the darkness, the baiting of New York City abolitionists, the verbal jousting in and outside the courtroom. 'In the chase his blood sang and glowed': the author doesn't flinch from showing us the workings of Ridgeway's deformed heart.

There's nothing unusual about switching point of view in a novel: it is a restraint-demanding technical feat that exposes many novices. At one level, Ridgeway's intervention is just a moment in a brilliant book that advertises fiction's power to make us morally complicit. Simply by attending to the details of Ridgeway's circumstances, the author gives the slave-catcher the humanity he denies to his kidnapped, abused, brutalised black quarry. I have no wish to increase my sympathy for slave-catchers or evil-doers of any kind, but the novel does it for me anyway. It is one of the demands that literature makes of us: you play this game, you're going to be in with the bad guys for at least some of the time. My first thought was that Whitehead had no right to be able to do this. How is it possible for a black American novelist to put us into the mind of a white man who catches runaway slaves for money? It was a trick, an act of conjury, a sleight of hand that seemed deliciously indecent. It asked me what a good book always does: where do my sympathies lie?

That moment in *The Underground Railroad* got me pondering this trick. I thought about times when I had been similarly morally upended by being placed in the shoes of people who do not think, feel or act like I do. In *Lolita*, Nabokov had put me into the mind of a paedophile, and challenged me to my core by showing me that the paedophile was a human being. Dostoevsky had done it with the murderer Raskolnikov in *Crime and Punishment*. It wasn't just about showing us the bad guy's point of view; it was about making damn sure we inhabited it. It worked for the good people too. I thought about all those times when brilliant writing has opened other worlds to me, when I have felt a little more understanding of a predicament for which my sympathy was untutored and underequipped, and thus not up to the task. This is what literature does. Novels are moral workouts precisely because they are no more likely – if they are halfway decent – to caricature the heinous than they are to cartoon-sketch the good.

And yet it is miraculous. I'm far from the first person to marvel at what Virginia Woolf called 'the immense persuasiveness of a mind which has completely mastered its perspective'. Every author strives for it; rookies make the mistake of not realising that a character's point of view has to be earned. When done well, literature puts us into suits of mental clothes that we usually don't try on. I call it a miracle, and yet it is a writer's bread and butter, a staple of what authors do. Toni Morrison puts it well in her recent essay collection, *The Origin of Others*. 'Narrative fiction,' she writes, 'provides a controlled wilderness, an opportunity to be and to become the Other. The stranger. With sympathy, clarity, and the risk of self-examination.' As a novelist, my technical curiosity makes me ask how this trick is even possible. As a reader, I want more of that exhilarating leap into another worldview.

As a human being, I feel that it's a trick the planet needs more of. It doesn't take much familiarity with the news to see that the world has become a more hate-filled place. In the US, the nonpartisan Center for the Study of Hate and Extremism reported a 20 per cent surge in hate crimes in nine metropolitan areas following the election of Donald Trump in 2016. In the UK, the popular vote to leave the European Union was followed by a substantial spike in racially and religiously aggravated offences, followed by further rises after the Westminster Bridge, Manchester Arena and London Bridge terrorist attacks. Home Office figures put the rise in hate crime between 2015–16 and 2016–17 at 29 per cent. These sad facts should come as no surprise: the political forces of Trumpism, Brexit and all shades of European nationalism have been nourished by campaigns that are less about issues than about distrust of the Other. I am just one of many people looking for a way to assuage a sense of powerlessness in the face of this tide of resentment. I am not alone in wanting to resist it. At workplace water coolers and in cafés and front rooms, the urge to do something, to try to effect some kind of change, is finding expression in varied and creative ways.

For me, it felt as though one answer might be right in front of our eyes. If literature does all these things, then it stands to reason that we should turn to it for respite. Who knows: perhaps the marvel it enacts every time a reader opens a book could even make the world a better place. In the months in which this project was gestating, I heard it said that books mattered more than ever. I wanted to ask why. I wanted to understand the tools that books give us for seeing reality from other points of view. It was this that really seemed to make the difference: not some worthy notion of empathy, but the miraculously practical efficiency with which literature expands the boundaries around a heart.

I make no claim that this is *specific* to literature. I imagine that everything I've said could apply equally well to any other art form; it's just that literature is the art form I know best. In one of my 'I have to do something' moments, I wondered whether I could find some writers to help me celebrate this special thing that writing does, and whether we could even turn it to some good.

The first step was to get in touch with some authors whom I hugely admire and who I knew shared my sense of outrage. I asked for pieces that would explore this special quality of literature, in whatever genres seemed to fit. I spoke to novelists, poets, essayists and specialists in narrative non-fiction. I asked people to experiment, and to switch away from their tried-and-tested formats if the instinct took them.

This anthology, *Others*, is the result. A feature of modern discussions of empathy is the idea that we have certain psychological and neural biases that shape our ability to see the world from other perspectives. As we all have brains and minds, I take this as self-evidently true. Some of the pieces here deal with psychology and neuroscience, but in ways that strive to be non-reductive. The deepest truth is the truth of human emotion and experience, and our present sciences can only give us a partial handle on that.

At least one finding from scientific research supports the ambition of this book. Social psychologists have shown that simply imagining having contact with individuals from another social group reduces prejudice towards that group. How, though, does that imagined contact come about? What are the motivations for it, particularly when the other group is ignored, patronised or silenced? Our brains are geared up for making the leap into different mental spaces, as decades of research into human 'social cognition' have shown. We come into the world ready to make sense of other people. But we need some grist to the mill, some fuel for our imagination, and some corrective to the forces that make us stick, habitually and jealously, to our own kind. I think these are some reasons why so many of us turn to the pages of a book.

There are risks in assuming that literature can unlock any and every point of view. As mentioned, good writers use this trick with discretion, sensitivity and humility. The pieces printed here ask how writers strive in various ways to take us beyond our own rooted viewpoints. There is an ethics of literature's miracle, and recent debates about cultural appropriation – defined as the adoption of the expressions and practices of a marginalised group by a more privileged one – focus our attention on it in important ways. Some authors have attracted criticism for portrayals of characters from under-represented groups who, some readers felt, should have been allowed to speak in their own voices. In its darkest moments, the debate sometimes feels like a struggle for the soul of literature. The writer Kenan Malik drew flak when, writing in the *New York Times*, he suggested that cultural appropriation is part of the fuel source for every art form. The novelist Lionel Shriver found herself at the centre of a storm in 2016 when she defended the rights of authors to write the stories of others. 'I would argue,' she stated in a speech published in the *Guardian*, 'that any story you can *make* yours is yours to tell, and trying to push the boundaries of the author's personal experience is part of a fiction writer's job.'

Responding to Shriver's speech in the same newspaper, a panel of professional writers pointed out some of the complexities she had missed. A sense of entitlement does not make for good fiction. One of the contributors to this volume, Kamila Shamsie, observed that writers need to 'understand that there are very powerful reasons for people to dispute your right to tell a story' – reasons that are historically and politically freighted. (Shriver attracted even greater opprobrium in 2018 when, in a separate intervention, she spoke out against steps to increase diversity in publishing.) Several of the 2016 *Guardian* contributors noted that writers who themselves spoke from marginal perspectives often, when entering a different imaginative territory, showed a deeper understanding of the individuals with whom they were sharing that space.

These feelings are starting to be reflected in changes in publishing's traditions. A recent movement in young people's fiction, #OwnVoices, has made a real difference in putting new and authentic voices onto bookshelves. But the logic of diversity is twisted if it is taken to mean that you have to be autistic, say, to write a character with autism, or that you have to have been a medieval peasant to create such a character in a novel. Writers of historical fiction, as much as any others, know that the need to respect the experience of one's characters reaches back into the past as much as it crosses geographical and cultural boundaries. The experience of human beings deserves human respect, whenever and wherever they happened to tread the planet. The *Guardian* contributors emphasised how the right to exercise one's imaginative powers has to be earned: through careful research and a sense of awe. Learn and listen, and use all the skills of the writer's craft, and you should be allowed the chance to try to do it well.

In this collection, and in the public events that have been associated with it, we have tried to explore what is involved in letting a reader inhabit a different worldview. How, when and under what conditions can – and should – writers try to master a perspective that is different from their own? Every writer will answer this differently, and all writers will have to work out for themselves which doors might swing open and what lines must never be crossed. But each one I have spoken to has defended it as a right that can, with the appropriate knowledge and sensitivity, be earned. The pieces in *Others* celebrate this magic trick, but also feel for its boundaries. Dare to imagine, they tell us, but do it with respect, and do it well. We need diversity and authenticity, but we also need to defend writers' right – and the responsibilities of their privilege – to launch themselves imaginatively across those divisions. Without it there would be no *Hamlet*, no *Beloved*, no *Mrs Dalloway*, no *Underground Railroad*.

Debates about cultural appropriation inevitably tend to coalesce around issues of racial and ethnic identity. Our failure to stand in other pairs of shoes is most catastrophic when it goes with imbalances of power. But great writing can also illuminate ordinary kinds of otherness, by taking us into points of view we might not otherwise have been able to enter: those moments when, thanks to the magic of words, people are less strange to each other, or when we glimpse something of the strangeness of our own selves. The pieces here consider otherness in a wide variety of its forms, from the dividing lines of politics and the anonymising forces of city life, through the disputed identities of disability, mental health and neurodiversity and the making and breaking of boundaries in the medical clinic and the asylum reception centre, to the endless battles that should have been won by now around social inequality. Some enact; others examine and explore. Most are new commissions; a few have been published before, but each of them deserves a new audience. Through it all, we have been focused on two complementary themes: how words on the page can break down barriers of understanding and imagination and propel us into other points of view, but also how they can show how we ourselves are 'other' to those we want to set apart as different, dangerous and unknowable. The greatest literature challenges us to recognise our own otherness; not just to understand how people out there are different to us, but how we are alien to them. Who are the others? The answer is simple. We are.

The anthology is in three sections. In the first, 'The Stranger Self', encounters with otherness are a force for unlocking truths about how we ourselves appear to the crowd. Preti Taneja's short story 'I, Jay' finds a helpline volunteer ambushed by memories of her own displacement. Rishi Dastidar's narrator reflects on his own response to something that might be casual racism in 'Is Queueing Politely Really the British Way?' Two poems in this section from Gillian Allnutt eavesdrop on a mind examining its own strangeness to itself. In 'Sounds of Blackness', Colin Grant writes about being black but not sounding it, and what it means for his own sense of identity. Will Storr's 'Original Sin' looks at the forces deep in the human psyche that draw it towards similar others and make it brazenly deny its own tribalism. In 'The Leavers of Boston', Edward Platt slips into the mindset of those who voted to leave the European Union in the Brexit referendum, and learns something about his own alienness to that slender majority. In 'Fast as Lightning', Peter Ho Davies traces the effects of a brutal racist attack on one of its protagonists' public loyalties and private memories.

The pieces in the second section, 'Not Like Me', explore how we react to people who don't conform to the default values of our culture. In Damian Barr's story 'Look Not with the Eyes', a young man is drawn into the world of a group of travelling actors, recognising the outlines of his own othering. Sam Guglani's prose poem 'Bodies' meditates on how the making and breaking of boundaries in the medical encounter push a doctor into a new confrontation of his own humanity. For the young boy in Sara Nović's story 'Things Unspoken', the arrival of a baby sister painfully reveals his society's attitude to those with a different sensory experience of the world. 'Excuse Me, but Your Otherness Is Showing' by Joanne Limburg attends to the task of making sense of one's life in the context of a late diagnosis of Asperger's. In 'We Are the Champions', Salena Godden examines her sister's experience of Williams Syndrome in relation to her own work in championing the voices of the marginalised and dispossessed. Tom Shakespeare's account of growing up with achondroplasia, 'A Short Story', challenges us about our ways of excluding people of different physical appearance, while Rachel Mann describes her search as a trans woman for community, pride and reconciliation in 'The Other Side of Gender'.

The final section, 'A Tardis of Souls', celebrates literature's trick of transporting us into other points of view, with pieces that look specifically to the need for understanding in a world riven by intolerance. Matt Haig's poem 'Others' shows a fragile self coming to terms with the fact that it is *it*, not the many-shaded humanity it fears, who is the alien one. Alex Preston's essay 'Choosing Sides' describes how a simple game of cricket shattered barriers in a xenophobic English community. Aamer Hussein's story 'Bridges' shows how the distances between us are stretched by the structures of the modern world, but also how we keep trying in our clumsy ways to span those gaps. The theme of the unknowability of others is picked up by Anjali Joseph in her piece 'In the Dark', in which a young man tries to understand the unreadable emotions of the woman who may become his wife. In 'Tuesday Lunch', Leila Aboulela puts us into the mind of a young girl dealing with the competing demands of the schoolroom, her family and her religion. Tiffany Murray touches on the solitude of a genius in her poem 'Emily Brontë's Bath'. A. L. Kennedy's story 'Point for Lost Children' finds a homeless woman unlocking the well-meaning kindness of a stranger who bears something of her own intolerable pain. In 'Are You Part-Something?' Louise Doughty describes how she has approached writing and speaking about her Roma heritage in the face of centuries-old prejudice and hatred. Kamila Shamsie's piece 'The A–Z of an Earthquake Zone' narrates the author's quest to find the humanity behind the numbers in the aftermath of a natural disaster. In 'Living in a Country of Words', Marina Warner describes the work she and her colleagues have been doing in exploring the cultural gift of storytelling with young migrants in Sicily. The theme of migration rounds off the collection, with Gillian Allnutt's 'Stars' and Noam Chomsky's piece on the refugee crisis, 'A Deep and Persistent Shame'.

It has been a privilege to work with these authors to bring you this collection. Profits from the book will be donated to Stop Hate UK, which works to raise awareness of hate crime and encourage its reporting, and Refugee Action, which provides advice and support to refugees and asylum seekers in the UK.

THE STRANGER SELF

I, Jay

Preti Taneja

Each of us will get the call. We are told this at the beginning. Listen, I think I am prepared. As the weeks go by, the others joke about it. They do not ask what it will be, because we know that we are not supposed to get too close. We learn this in empathy class. I wonder what I will do, when the call comes for me. I say I am ready.

It happens on my fourth four-hour shift: week four. The biros in the tin cup are red, blue, black. I scribble a tangle of hair on the page. I clean the ear piece and put the mouth piece to my lips. The answer forms are waiting. The supervisor is at the main call desk, captain of us.

There is sunlight in the room, and outside the tall windows the high street is busy. It is a Friday afternoon in the month of July. A procession of very clean shop windows show white dummies draped in shweshwe; that is the fashion in London right now. One can buy this fabric at a better price in the local market. Originally it is from South Africa. I know because I asked the lady seller in her stall. I want to buy some fabric for myself. I want to sew a summer dress.

As I come to the call centre I can feel that English excitement in the air. It is the end of the week. Release for office workers. Later there will be doorways of old men sleeping, overlooked by spreading trees.

I take the green chair, the one I find most comfortable. The centre is like an office. There is not one natural thing in it. Plants are plastic and walls were painted white. Purple has been used for the chairs and carpet.

A soft wall of grey boards separates me from the others. Today, there are no notices pinned up. No warning of repeat pranksters, or special timed appointments for me.

Buses go by and shake our floor; each time they do, I feel shock.

One of the others has brought a tub of small chocolate cakes. It is on the desk over there. I cannot indulge. My breakfast was masala polenta. It is a good meal for such days. The shift is going easy – a call about school stress, a teenager with a problem parent. A group of older boys shouting down the phone: among them one confesses shame at his bad skin. I have learned a lot about my own sense of humour in the past four weeks. The others never ask why I sometimes laugh after calls. And now the light on my phone centre flashes. I press *receive*. The voice of a Younger slides into my ear.

He does not say his name and I do not ask. He loves Madonna, he says, but Beyoncé is his bestilicious. I ask him to repeat this word and I write it down. He says he wants get up early to watch live-stream Coachella. I do not know what that is, but Beyoncé I know, and he says 'Emotions' by Destiny's Child is his tune. And oh, it is in my recall. Maya. She used to hum a phrase of it. Now this young man hums and he is not her. She sang those words and danced in our room. I'm cry a river, la la la vos océan.

I gather myself. OK, Destiny's Child, how old are you? I ask. He says he is fourteen. He has a light voice. I ask to know what he wants to talk about today. He says, insides. OK. Sure. I frequently get boys who want help with protection. Once I stopped the office silent by describing what to do. The others said it was wonderful to listen to me. Why? Because when they get those questions they feel some reticence. But it is all about lips and fingers – punch the phone and speak the words; if the caller wants to know how to use a condom then I am able to advise. I say, take a banana and the protection. Now pinch the end. Now roll the plastic down the banana. Have patience. Try again. There is no shame in that. How do you know if the child is ready and that you should answer? Because they call, they ask. Because that was not *the* call, it was just one among many.

We agree that I will refer to him as DC. I tell him I am Jay. He wants to know about me. I am not permitted to give any details. He says *my sister left me*. I am cold. A feeling aches behind my eyes.

There is no back-story, only story.

This is what we learn in the first training as I sit with the others in a small grey room. The space is plain as the processing centre, but there are cream biscuits on offer. And there are information sheets on the walls, showing two empty chairs side by side, and question marks between them. *Empathy is sitting next to, not opposite.* At the bottom of the sheet is the number for children to call and speak to us. It is a free number, one can call from any kind of phone. I have to ask what 'back-story' is. I write the phrase down in my book.

We are asked in turn: Why are you here? The others look at Sandra, and I am pleased to see a woman similar in age to me. Yet, she laces her hair around her fingers when she talks, as if she is a young girl. Her hair is fine and yellowish. She talks on local radio, she says, and is an experienced call-taker, live on air, life lived live, people need that. She says she has an assistant to find the next record, the one that will get people smiling again. I think that must be something, to have an assistant. Sandra likes to help people, and so she wanted to do more, she retired from secretarial work and now she is on the radio, but there is still so much time in the day. People tell her she is a good listener. People say that, she says.

Mike has a grown-up son. His wife works as a lawyer in a big estate agent's – the one with most of the green and yellow boards all over, he laughs, she *owns* London. He is wearing a pinstripe suit and all, he looks like the white men who will congregate outside bars in the city on weeknight evenings when I am on my way to char: yes, I am a charlady, this is also a new word for me. The men fill the street corners, one has to cross to the opposite side; their fulsome voices rise and spread into the air like flesh on warm summer days, and oh, those gatherings we all hold dear, everyone with someone, together. There is a French woman, Vanessa, an artist with a studio space not far from the town hall, she tells us. She is like her short friend Emiliana, who says she was born in France but in her heart she is the true child of her parents' island. Now Vanessa and the short Emiliana live together here in London. She has a name I cannot imagine, her mother country is the opposite direction, and further from here than mine. Vanessa and Emiliana are beautiful together. They sometimes hold hands. They have chosen to give their energy to this cause. It moves me. Yet, in the training weeks they do not come close to any of us, especially they keep out from me.

These are some of the others.

I cannot hold on to my voice when they want to know why am I here. I try to say: it is a free course. I want to learn the skills. It is good to stay out of the shared house for a while. The library is closing early. I want to talk to people. I pass much of my time on my own.

There are people I can help, I say.

The trainer is an older lady called Rosie. She tells the others that I have 'recently arrived'. But this is not my job description. Here, I am a volunteer, while learning everyday English to add to what I know. And nods all round. The others respect Rosie and her words.

I do not offer my story. This is not group therapy as some in my shared house attend. We are to learn to listen. I offer to make a batch of tea. That is how I was brought up. Daughter do. It has stood me in good stead in new situations. The processing centre. The shared house. The others do not come to give a hand. People enjoy having a cup of tea made for them.

DC, I say. Who is with you? Are you alone?

Are you? he asks.

I put my head around the board and count the others. Yes, I tell him.

In the training weeks, twelve of us go to ten, because two of them just can not make it to every session, sorry. Then to eight, because Anna, a laughing woman who was always tardy and telling stories about how her Lucy has been in the hospital again for bumps and bruises (because little ones' bones are so soft aren't they, and Lucy is prone to tumbles) loses her composure on the training session for domestic violence. She says her mother taught her that lemon juice is good for fresh bruises. She does not come back for the next session. Neither does Mike, we are never told why.

In our final training we are given points. I, Jay, get the most for empathy, even though often I have no partner pair and sit quite apart. As the others watch, Rosie gifts me a pink beauty bag. Inside is a roll-on, a toothbrush and a tube of mint toothpaste. I want to say, what about the eye mask, the ear plugs and the pen? These are the important items, the ones that I truthfully want. It is hard to sleep in the shared house, and the noise is all night. And all of us can use an extra pen. Rosie is a kind-faced woman, the sort who over-smiles at me. What does she smile like that for all the time? I think she must feel very blessed. Her cardigan is expensive. She says the gift bag is for doing so well. She holds it up in her hands as if to protect her heart from me. The others are still watching. I say – *Thank you*. She smiles at me. The others clap.

This is when I know I will graduate to the phones.

DC says he stayed behind today because he has fallen and bruised his arm. Did someone hit you or push you? I ask. He laughs. Will you come and rescue me? He sounds younger than before. I rub out 14 and use a biro to write 11 on his form. Tell me, I say. How are you? All right, he says. But I can't open the door, I've hurt my arm, I've locked myself in and I don't know what to do. It's your emotions, he sings, taking you over.

Pain, a game of it, is all between us. Now his talk happens to my bones, not to my ears. I am tired and there is nothing to eat. There is nothing to play with. I cannot get out, everyone has left me. I do not know when they are coming back. The building is shaking. The soft walls tremble. I can hear how frightened the child is. I want to hold my hand over my heart but I cannot move.

My own voice asks, what can you see?

There is a high window, like being on a boat.

Now, I think this boy is making believe. I am reminded by my training that truth is not our purpose here. Not my role to catch him out. Children call for some reason, and wrap it up in a story. Fear. There is no story, I think. Only back-story. So, I stay with him. DC. I say. Tell me about your day.

This is my mistake.

I play with my sister in the morning, he says. His voice so like voices I have known. I look up and around, no one can see me. My eyes are waterlogged and drowning. Did your sister leave you in the house and tell you not to move? Did your father bring you to another country and leave you with your uncle? We come here to this country and there are so many of us. We are held. And then we are sent in different directions. We cannot keep together.

I have locked myself in and there is no one here.

But you have TV, I say. Live stream.

He says, I wish I did.

I think of that room, with that child inside. Imagine calling the number and I, Jay answer with questions about what your father did, about how he left you alone with some kind strangers. Remember the songs, along long highways. The second camp, where hours passed. Always cold and tired. Watching boys play football in mud. Boats and food trucks, there were so many men. There is kindness there, and we run around in the mornings. I have a pair of diamanté earrings. I learn a little of the language. Before that, what? Maya, in our bedroom at home. I recall the smell of her hair in my face, in our bed, and the softness of our pillows.

I should get the supervisor. I need to bring the call to an end, because my hands are shaking. I am lost for words. The others are not looking at me, everyone is on their own, and I am getting the call.

DC? I say. Are you telling the truth? Mistake follows mistake. Do you know where you live? He repeats only the details. A room and a mirror and a bed. A phone he has from his sister, who is gone without him. I know he is embellishing. I, Jay am the sister who got away. There was no way to communicate our flight. DC can hear me, not breathing. He sighs. As if the story has been told so many times, it gets too simple in the repeating. Yet nothing changes. Did he say that? Why are we here? My work is to listen. This is not my country of origin. Why am I here?

There are moments in training when I role-play with the others. I am the caller, and one of them is the volunteer. We change places. I discover that someone fears the call about eating issues, and that someone does not want to get girls who are persuadable. Mr Mike (before he left) tells me that he is likely to receive a call from the boy with feelings for his teacher; his own son, he says, was used like that, what could he do? Rosie said, The call won't be like that. It will come

21

from offside, a curve ball. I had no idea what her meaning was. Just keep calm, she said, continuez.

The bed cover is purple, the walls yellow. The people around told me to stay quiet, be good, my father would want that. I was not alone but one of many. This morning I made polenta and two fried for breakfast in the shared house. I have lived without Maya for years. She got left behind. We left her behind. She was hiding and we had to go. DC sings *that he is caught*. The next words are *up*, and *sorrow*. Around the walls are posters showing empty chairs, question marks and the phone number he has called. The time clock on the phone says 40:35 – time I must end our session. Even if I do, the child will still be there. Even if I do, I will still be here. DC? Are you safe? What do you need from me? Just listen, he says. And sings. Keep calm, continuez.

Continuity is too hard. I cannot find a way to breathe. DC is talking, telling me about his friends, and what he is missing at school. Swimming, he says, although he is afraid of the jump in, he has a sense of imbalance when he thinks about it. I understand that – I must end the call. He sings again. There was always someone singing as we walked through the city, there was so much dust. We went to school through it. It is true that in London I have a strong sense of home. The silence of the others means I do not know myself. DC says – there is no one coming. I, Jay must help him get out. But how? The protocol is that I keep him talking, decide if emergency services are needed, stay on the call to wait for them.

I am the one who got away. I am in the grip of it. The others are beginning to notice and look at me. Yet, none of them approaches.

22

The boy sings *Emotions*, and there is Maya's voice, nestled inside his. I begin to hum, I cannot help it. I'm crying. *A river la la la vos océan* – Where are you? I say, too loudly. Do you know where you are?

DC breaks the call.

Now the others are all around me, leaving their booths to stand with me. I see their faces through my tears, all appear to be one face.

Jay, says the face. The others separate into who they are.

Jay, says Vanessa, again.

The call, I say. It got me. I laugh. It is unlike my other laugh.

Rosie takes my call-form from me, and reads *bestilicious*. She frowns and moves away. Purple bed cover, yellow walls. No name, no details in one hour. Something about the ocean, and Maya. I am afraid I will lose this opportunity that I have trained for. I am afraid Rosie will not allow me to come back. These are child callers. They need us to be safe.

Rosie says, it's OK, we've had this one before. He's just a lonely boy. Likes to sing down the phone. It happens to all of us. Take a break, Jay. It's Friday. Have a cake. Rosie holds out the tub of small cakes. She brought them today. Sandra, she says. Go make us all a cuppa char.

I blink at the word. I will not come back here. How can I? Grief remains inside.

The others move closer to me as if they know what I am thinking. Vanessa produces a scented handkerchief from her cotton sleeve, a lace relic, perhaps it belonged to her grandmother. She gives it to me. The faint smell of her perfume is flowers. Emiliana puts her hand on my shoulder. It is the first time she has touched me. Her

23

fingers are slim and she shines her nails. I do this too. I put my hand over hers so she can see this. We blend together. The smell of the handkerchief, the feel of our hands make me aware of my own skin, the strength of my own bones in a way I have not since I left Maya behind. Maya, I say. Elle était ma soeur. She was my sister.

They nod, these two women, and they stand either side of me. Vanessa is wearing a pearl necklace. Emiliana is so short. But something about them is so similar that one can only feel different when near them.

For the first time, I feel that less.

Sandra comes back. Kettle's on, she says.

We are a motley crew, says Rosie. Aren't we? That's why we are here.

I, Jay stand up and look at the smiling, nodding women. I do not fully know what this phrase means. I have not learned it yet, but I will.

From 2001 to 2003, the writer trained and then volunteered as a counsellor for a national helpline.

Is Queueing Politely Really the British Way?

Rishi Dastidar

D- at work's birthday, and he is rounding people up to come with him for an impromptu lunch 'somewhere'. We get outside of the front door of the office, we being me and T- and B- and D-, to discover that joining the four of us will be C- (or is it A-?), who is freelancing with us this week. He is wearing a fleece jacket, black, with a vivid red spider on the left breast pocket.

> *These temporary alliances*
> *I keep making; and yet*
> *I don't seem to win the battle.*

On the walk down to find food it's clear C- is having trouble attaching himself to a conversation. Not something that is being helped by the four of us – the very image that the advertising and design community likes to think that it is, encompassing two genders, two sexualities, two nationalities, three levels of educational achievement (let's not talk about our ages) – being cliquey and only speaking about office things there's no way he'd ever get or that could be even close to comprehensible without a lot of explanation that no one is actually ever going to be bothered to give. I half expect at points for him to give up and drift off.

> *My nightmare is*
> *being on the outside –*
> *and he remains in*

But he doesn't, and we arrive at the 'somewhere', the pizza place where there is a bit of a queue, but not much and it is moving. There are two tills and people are going through, ordering, getting their clickers which will let them know when their food is ready. He is standing behind me at this point. The till on the left becomes free, and I start to move towards it as I am next in line, but before I have even got off my first step he has moved ahead of me and is at that till ordering.

And I can't help but feel slighted here. That of course he would go ahead of me, instead of waiting for the till he was supposed to wait for.

Is this because we – I – haven't been inclusive enough, not sensitive enough to what is actually shyness, and not tried hard enough to welcome him in? I thought I'd been friendly earlier in the week.

Is this a gag I'm missing out on? But there's no look back, no hand up in apology. No wink.

Yes, it is rank opportunism, but it is more than that, I am already telling myself. Because he is older. Whiter. Because even though he is a freelancer and not part of the gang that I am part of, he still outranks me in some way. Because he is entitled to. Because he can. Because he doesn't see me as someone he should ever be expected to wait behind.

I am surprised at how much this cuts me, even though it is a nano-moment, the business of nano-moments, as the other till becomes free in a matter of seconds so I can order. I don't mention it to anyone when I sit down at the table while we wait for the pizzas to be ready.

> *Or is the nightmare*
> *being cut out when*
> *you were inside?*

Then part of me starts thinking that actually I was expecting something like this to happen, and I'm not sure why (I'm not vocalising any of this, by the way, over lunch – I am ravenous enough to not actually engage with much other than the pizza [fully loaded, all the meats] in front of me). But even calories can't push away all my thoughts.

Maybe it was some form of barely visible revenge, or if not, an attempt by someone who was feeling excluded to not feel excluded, and he did the thing that was most natural to him so that he wouldn't feel excluded, which was to take out his lack of status on me, the person he perceived as either having next to no status, or an unwarranted status, certainly in relation to him, certainly in terms of being above him socially in this context, even if the context is – literally – *I work with these people every day and you do not.*

A micro-aggression. The tiniest of hostilities. A deniable slight. We've all done it. Haven't we? A gesture of impatience at someone holding us up on the street as we try to get somewhere. A *sotto voce* retort as someone bores us. A laugh at a mean comment, then a guilty sucking up of the guffaw, as if that absolves us. *We've all been unthinking, unwittingly cruel.*

> *But even if you shouldn't do it,*
> *wouldn't you do it? Why should*
> *he be in my place?*

Presumably there was also an alpha male territory thing going on, and really, it seems so silly and futile to even think about trying to fight for and/or over a patch of land which is by definition only ever going to be temporary anyway. *What sort of rush are you in when we are all going to be going back to the same place at the same time?*

Even better, I think he thinks that he pulled off this little victory over me without me noticing, like he was so smooth and slick – I bet he gave himself a mini fist-pump mentally for that moment, and then promptly forgot about it.

> *A moment, erased,*
> *because it was only*
> *a moment for me.*

Of course for me it was a moment that lasted longer, because it was a moment in which *I* was erased.

Stranger

Gillian Allnutt

Who is this stranger lies here by me
Who, as my heart, has turned me over to God unheard?
Than my own words, stranger
Than my bed of words.

It is always worth remembering the stranger in myself. It is a question of courtesy,
the old medieval sort, and of hospitality; and a way of being open, discerningly, to
all comers. Worth remembering that whatever I block or shut out in myself, I shall
also shut out in others.

Sounds of Blackness

Colin Grant

As a teenager, Bob Marley, the light-skinned son of a black woman and a white man, was so determined to demonstrate which side of the racial divide he identified with that he regularly insisted that his girlfriend Rita run black shoe polish in his hair so that it seemed coarser, blacker and more African. The stakes were high. Rastas in Trenchtown, Jamaica's most forbidding ghetto, would open ceremonies which Bob Marley attended with the chant, 'death to the white man and his brown allies'. Marley's actions weren't just aesthetic; they were existential. Ultimately the force-ripe youth realised it was necessary to assimilate to his surroundings, to pick a side and put down a marker of belonging. But can you still choose to belong if you are not accepted?

I grew up in a black West Indian family on Farley Hill, one of the council estates on the fringes of Luton in the 1960s and 70s. It was heavily populated with Irish families. Our neighbours, and my friends, were Flynns, Dunns, McLoughlins and O'Learys. My fondest moments were always those when Luton Irish were down a player on the Sunday league, and I'd be asked to don a green and white football shirt to join lads whose parents had migrated from Doolin, Cork, Galway. On those occasions, for an hour or so, I'd undergo a conversion, and differences between us (not that there were many) disappeared; I was Irish.

My family gravitated towards the Irish, in part because of a shared antipathy towards the English. The English (never the British in our minds) had subjugated black Caribbean people for 400 years, but the Irish topped that; they'd been under the Englishman's heel for 800 years. If anything, eavesdropping on their conversations, the Irish pain seemed rawer than ours; they had neither forgotten nor forgiven their hosts.

There can't have been more than half a dozen Caribbean families scattered across the thousand or more homes that made up the estate. I sensed my father, Bageye, liked it that way, although he never said as much. Bageye had grown up in Jamaica, a society ordered around shades of colour, a pigmentocracy with fair-skinned people at the top. Bageye with his darker hue would have found himself on the bottom rung. But in Luton, on Farley Hill, no one knew him. He could start again; Farley Hill was a blank canvas. Until one day, in their wisdom, the council decided to move in another West Indian family right next door to us. I suspect the council and social workers believed they were being benevolent, but my father fumed. We stood behind him peeking round the curtain as the new neighbours arrived with a vanload of furniture. 'Imagine this,' said Bageye, 'I travel four thousand miles to get away from these people and who do they put next door?'

I wasn't startled by my father's sourness; we'd grown used to hearing tales of the nasty naygars (niggers) letting the side down.

It was only when I heard him repeat the anecdote with his West Indian friends later on that I realised Bageye considered himself to be joking. I wasn't so sure.

I was determined to extinguish that self-loathing side of West Indian life that I'd witnessed growing up. But it was complicated because, at the age of eleven, after much scrimping and saving, my parents sent me to a just-about-affordable private school twenty miles away. It meant that my interactions with other West Indians became more limited. I wasn't exposed so readily to the harsh but comedic attitudes West Indians took with each other; and consequently there were fewer opportunities to develop the social skills to address them.

The problem faced by black people at the start of the twentieth century, argued the black political activist Marcus Garvey, was the problem of perception. Garvey was not just analysing how the white man perceived the black man as a degraded human being; he was musing also on the way black people saw each other.

At his peak, in 1920s Harlem, Garvey gave weekly speeches to thousands of followers, members of the Universal Negro Improvement Association (UNIA). A silver-tongued orator, Garvey tapped into the dreams and aspirations of a downtrodden people; numerous admirers testified that when Garvey spoke of unity it was as if they were hearing their own thoughts articulated. The cry may have been unity, but unity there never was. Rather, there were fissures, fractures and varying emphases between black people (which Freud would have characterised as the 'narcissism of minor differences') on the best way forward.

Broadly, two camps emerged in North America (which were

subsequently replicated throughout the diaspora) during the period of Garvey's greatest prominence: his own UNIA, a bottom-up organisation of working-class black people, and the National Association for the Advancement of Coloured People (NAACP) led by W. E. B. Du Bois, whose movement attracted the so-called 'talented tenth', the fair-skinned tertiary-educated 10 per cent of the black population whom Du Bois envisioned as an intellectual avant-garde.

The problems within the black population emerged with the relative success and confidence of an aspiring black middle class who increasingly moved out from the black conurbations where doctors and lawyers had lived cheek-by-jowl with poorer blacks, plumbers and refuse collectors.

Growing up amongst black working-class people, but sent to a private school, it was possible to cross over from one class to another without realising it. Education was a bridge along which I assumed I'd be able to travel back and forth; it was definitely not, as far as I was concerned, a means to cross into the citadel and draw up the bridge after me. Yet you cannot legislate for how others see you. For some, somewhere along the line, my appearance and my voice must have changed. Apparently, I no longer did such a good impression of a black person. I was less and less likely to pass for black even when my skin colour offered a visual cue.

'These West Indians make an awful racket, don't they?' said the commuter, half turning towards me. I was surprised by his intervention. We had stood isolated from each other on an otherwise empty platform at Harpenden, a leafy suburban village, one stop up the train line from Luton, where I lived. Granted it was dark and I was in my private school uniform, but surely he could see that I, too, was black and probably of West Indian origin. He sighed at the porters in their cubby-hole at the end of the platform. Oblivious to his disapproval, they continued their game of dominoes.

Although no offensive words were uttered by the commuter, I detected a racial element in his antipathy to the men who could have been my uncles or at least peers of my father. He had been quite proper in his use of language, but though he had simply said 'West Indians' he'd managed to convey something entirely different. The term 'West Indians' had been a proxy for an unnamed word. I said nothing, and forty years on I still carry a sense of guilt for that silence. It might even have fuelled my ambition to write myself back into my colour.

On publishing my first book, *Negro with a Hat*, a biography of Marcus Garvey, I took part in a phone-in. The host, reassuringly, was a former pastor and perfectly polite. On the line to the BBC I listened as the first caller cut through the airwaves and spoke to the host. 'I just want to say...' The caller could barely contain his fury. He had no question; he just wanted to make a point. 'I resent the fact,' said the caller, 'that the publishers got a white man to write a book on Garvey.'

'What makes you think,' I interrupted, 'that I'm white?'

The caller seemed taken aback. 'Well, you don't sound black!'

I clearly hadn't worked enough on how I was supposed to sound. But what relation does the sound of your voice play to who you are? If you lose your black voice, have you lost your blackness? James

Baldwin encountered the same dilemma when, living in Switzerland, armed with two Bessie Smith records and a typewriter, he attempted to write his first novel. 'I realized that I had not always talked – obviously I hadn't always talked – the way I had forced myself to learn how to talk,' said Baldwin in an interview. 'I had to find out what I had been like in the beginning, in order, just technically as a writer, to re-create Negro speech.' Baldwin's solution was to play the Bessie Smith records every day. 'A lot of the book is in dialogue, you know, and I corrected things according to what I was able to hear when Bessie sang.'

There's a clinic in York which specialises in helping people who are losing their voice, mostly through some kind of pathology such as cancer of the larynx. A patient is able to 'bank' her/his voice, to record a number of phrases, building up a catalogue of sounds so that, when the voice is eventually lost, it can be restored to the patient through a keyboard and synthesiser. Many people, though, don't want their original voice back; they're disturbed by the sound; it leaves them with an existential angst. A number of volunteers have donated their voices such that the clinic has a library to draw on and offer to the voiceless.

Outside of the voice clinic the researchers conducted a survey into how people felt about their voices. I wrote down that my black voice had been educated out of me. 'So you don't like the sound of your voice? But you have a lovely voice,' said the woman conducting the survey. 'No, if I was to lose my voice, I wouldn't want it back,' I said, telling her I'd want the voice of Bob Marley or Marcus Garvey, a voice that suggested a richness of experience, integrity and authenticity. 'What do you mean by authenticity?' she asked. 'Blackness,' I answered.

In the 1970s and 80s many of my peers had been radicalised by Garvey's writings. I didn't come to the party until much later – the latter-day equivalent to a tourist with a typewriter, compared to a whole subgroup of people who were 'living' Marcus Garvey, whose teaching gave shape and meaning to their lives.

The BBC phone-in was a prelude to what was to come; a stream of black activists followed in subsequent weeks who considered me suspicious, not fully black. The Ligali Front (a collection of activists) bid its members assemble at my first reading of the Garvey book. As reported on its forum, I had announced my 'Uncle Tom' credentials with the title of my book, *Negro with a Hat.*

That night at the Marcus Garvey library in Haringey, their temper might have been judged by the blogger who wrote: 'If Dem Diss Marcus Dem Must Die!' And in the estimation of Ligali's Brother Olatunji, Chief Officer Politics Department, the title *Negro with a Hat* for a biography of Garvey was akin to calling a book on Jinnah *Paki in a Suit.*

Just inside the atrium of the library, a dull-faced punter, vacillating over whether to borrow the new biography, seemed to brighten as I walked in. His eyes flicked between me and the author's photo on the flap of the jacket.

'Oh, is you,' he burped through Guinness breath. 'You brave! Never expect you would-a come.'

His tone was worrying, but the first signs, as the crowd assembled, appeared promising. A neatly turned-out man wearing a suit was the first to take a front-row seat. His clean fingernails and starched shirt (a dead ringer for Sidney Poitier in *Guess Who's Coming to Dinner*) immediately marked him out as an ally. The Ligali Front were particularly vexed by the *Telegraph* reviewer's conclusion that Garvey was a 'Jamaican David Brent' – and clearly held me personally responsible for the review. Sister Nzingha had helpfully photocopied the article and proceeded to hand it out. If the book was a slug, here was the slime.

The crowd were united in their disgust. Shouting above the din, I called upon Sidney Poitier to enlighten us all with his reflections. He started piously mumbling something about top shelves, naked women and pornography; he knew what to expect from titles such as *Mayfair* and *Men Only*; the same was true of *Negro with a Hat*. Sidney's assessment prompted a chorus of 'Yes man, respect. Respect!' Above the squall of indignant voices someone helpfully suggested we needed a moderator. No sooner had I agreed than Sister Nzingha started to drag her chair towards the stage. A knot of excitement was finally freed in her unfurling dreadlocks. 'Right,' she bellowed, 'we'll have a question from Brother Gumba then Sister Serene. You can follow Brother Zion. I'll come to you in a minute Sister Kay...'

'Hold on, wait a second,' I interrupted, 'what about, erhh, someone else we haven't already heard from?' Ken, the most coherent critic, answered: 'The problem is, Colin, you're coming across as arrogant.' Perhaps, suggested Ken, I could give away a couple of copies of the book. After all, no one had read the biography; it was impossible to gauge my motives. The talk came to an end. I sat at a tiny desk with my writer's autograph pen ready. The crowd stormed to the front. The first review copy was claimed, tucked under the armpit of Sister Nzingha; the next copy similarly disappeared without an exchange of money, and then one more, then a couple of others, until finally none remained.

That was almost a decade ago. The Ligali Front is now at the helm of the Black Lives Matter movement in the UK. If I was writing Garvey's biography today I don't think I would have had the nerve to call the book *Negro with a Hat.* Self-harming battles amongst allies and activists have not been uncommon throughout history but I'm sure that the Ligali Front would have been bemused to learn that some of my BBC colleagues drew little distinction between us.

For more than twenty years I have worked as a radio producer in the BBC. Over those years I have been lulled into thinking that no one pays any attention to my colour; I am not a black producer but simply a producer. Occasionally, the myth is punctured.

A couple of years ago, as I ambled towards a workshop in Broadcasting House, I passed a fellow producer in a different department from mine (but known to me by sight). He stopped and turned back to me and said: 'Are you looking for a computer?'

I looked around the open-plan room and observed that not one of the twenty or so staff in that department was black. I didn't really know what he meant and mumbled that no, I was on my way to a workshop. I noticed a few things we had in common: he was probably about my age; we both wore neatly pressed long-sleeved shirts (mine was plain, his pinstriped); and we both had soft southern voices – his only slightly more clipped than mine.

A few minutes later I was still puzzling over the comment *Are you looking for a computer?* when, looking through the workshop window into the open-plan office, I saw the producer, now at his desk, with a man from computer support attending him. A hot flush of recognition washed over me that my fellow producer had mistaken me for a technician from IT.

I was disturbed, not at being cast with other black workers at the lower end of the professional ladder, but rather by the blinkered assumption that the exalted position of producer had to be filled by someone who was white. For that moment I, the producer, was invisible. And when the time came, as it would in the future, when my white colleague scaled the professional ladder to the position of editor and had to appoint new producers, would he be able to visualise a producer who did not look like him? Would the scales of prejudice suddenly fall from his eyes?

Throughout my childhood, I had been taught by my parents who weathered daily slights at the hands of white Englishmen that, when it came to my turn, I should take it on the chin, pull up the collar on my coat, as it were, and walk on. But I am tired. By not acting on a transgression do you invalidate the experience? Are you not, in effect, kicking the problem down the street for the next black person who follows you?

At times when my siblings have celebrated and taken vicarious pleasure from the good things that have come my way in life, they have rolled out a favourite expression: 'You gone clear! Dem can't touch you now.' But to walk through life as a black person in this country is to have a giant elastic band strapped across your chest that you pull on; it stretches and stretches with the years but doesn't snap, and then one day it catapults you right back to where you started – on a cold night on a sleepy platform in Harpenden with a commuter for whom you are all but invisible.

I could have drawn on any number of my back catalogue of humiliations in writing this account. Whilst the BBC embarrassment was no greater than others, it should pique because it added to the flood of mini insults and micro-aggressions which finally threatened to break the dam of feigned indifference I had spent decades erecting. I had not gone clear.

But before I called out my white doppelgänger it was important to admit that though I am black I am also privileged, and to pause to consider, for instance, the transgressions endured routinely by my black friends in BBC computer support; to ask myself: 'I wonder who they are mistaken for?'

The temptation is to default to defensiveness, to consider your victimhood greater than others; that there are hierarchies of suffering, an inversion of the social order with black people on top. But it's worth considering the fact that you are not alone; that there's the possibility, for example, of intersectionality. I found the most common response about the anecdote of being mistaken for 'somebody else' at the BBC was from female friends and associates who said words to the effect of 'welcome to my world; this is how it mostly feels to be a woman'.

Recently, along with the Yoruba/Irish poet Gabriel Gbadamosi, I was commissioned to host a talk on the psychology of oppression. When it came to the decision about what to call the talk, I reflected on Gabriel's dual heritage, and travelled back in time and thought of my friends on Farley Hill. Finally, Gabriel and I settled on the title which we hoped might check our weariness about the one step forwards, two steps backwards dance of progress towards non-discrimination, and at the same time encourage empathy for others: 'Tired of being black? Try being Irish'.

Original Sin

Will Storr

It was in a barrio outside Guatemala City that I first came to understand the reality and nature of original sin. I was a guest of Rigo Garcia, a twenty-nine-year-old who'd suffered the misfortune of being born and raised in Peronia, one of the most dangerous neighbourhoods in one of the most deadly cities in the world. We were driving to his small concrete and breeze-block home, which jutted out in a maze of others up the side of a steep hill. As we entered his barrio, we were nodded through by a trio of rangy adolescents who were leaning against the bonnet of a truck. Instinctively, I grabbed for my camera. 'Don't take their photograph,' Rigo hissed, as our car rolled past. 'Don't even look at them. They've killed people.'

The nascent gang had existed for about four years, Rigo explained later, as we settled in the relative safety of his house. 'You have to kill someone if you want to join them, as an initiation. You saw those memorials outside?' We'd passed a row of handmade steel crosses on the steps up the hill, on which names and dates had been roughly painted. 'It was those boys who killed them, outside the house.' The deceased were two brothers and a cousin, ages seventeen, sixteen and thirteen. The killings were pre-emptive. One gang of kids had come to believe the other gang of kids would've murdered them, if they didn't strike first. And was this belief correct? 'Of course,' said Rigo. And what would've happened to me, just now, if I'd arrived on their territory without you? 'They would've killed you.'

Rigo told me about his childhood in Peronia. As a boy, he'd loved flying home-made kites that he and his friends would craft out of plastic they'd find in the street and sticks from the ravine. When he was fourteen, a youth boxing club opened up. It was popular enough that the club's owners ran two daily groups, one in the morning, one in the afternoon. Soon, a friendly rivalry formed between them. Matches were arranged. Fights were fought and lost. Boasting became goading; goading became threatening. Some of the youngsters started coming to class with bats and knives to defend themselves from potential attacks. One day, the afternoon group stormed the morning group's lesson. They'd built *hechiza*, home-made guns, from pipes and the legs of television stands. And so it was that, as naturally as air becomes wind, these individuals had formed groups and those groups became rivals and those rivals had entered a state of tribal conflict. This is what we do, our species. We're groupish. And not harmlessly, like starlings or sheep or shoals of mackerel, but violently. This is our original sin.

We're born like this. Most of us are lucky enough not to be enculturated in an environment such as Peronia, that allows that monster to run so freely. But make no mistake, it is in you. The only two species on earth that live in groups that go to war with other groups, and inflict acts of nightmarish barbarity upon members of their own kind simply for being a member of a different group, are us and the chimpanzee. The chimpanzee is one of our closest evolutionary cousins and one with whom we share a common ancestor. This strongly suggests that this impulse, that's so stunningly rare in nature, is embedded deep within us and has been for perhaps millions of years. Optimists sometimes attempt to release us from our sin by arguing that we're equally related to the bonobo, who doesn't behave like this, so *maybe it's not in our biology after all*. But this just begs the question: how come we do it then? Over and over and over again? Good for the bonobo, who evolved in a different direction. Not so our other primate cousins, who patrol the perimeters of their territory in gangs and, when encountering the 'other', rip off arms, tear off testicles and gulp down blood. And us, of course, of whom tribal conflict killed 160 million in the twentieth century alone, whether by genocide, political oppression or war.

For decades, psychologists have been researching what's sometimes called the 'minimal group effect'. The question is, what are the minimal conditions necessary for human brains to start thinking groupishly – to start being biased towards their own 'in' group and prejudiced towards the 'out'? What do you imagine those minimal conditions might be? Does this mode of thinking require some sort of propaganda; tales of the 'others'' wrong? Does it require uniforms? A flag? A rabble-rousing leader? Perhaps some sort of competitive framework would do it: two football teams; two sets of puffing villagers pulling at ends of a rope at a village fair? Or something deeper? A shared skin colour? A shared national history?

A shared family tree? In fact, it requires none of that. All you have to do, to get humans to start unconsciously elevating their own kind over the 'other', is to put a bunch of them in a room and randomly split them in two. Then watch it all begin, subtly at first, but quick: halos on you and yours, devil's horns and sulphur-stink coming off that lot over there.

We all know how it feels to think like that. No doubt you've felt it at times. That's the monster in you, the neural expression of your original sin. That primeval ape, with its sharp fangs, bloody fingers and almighty strength, really exists and, when you think groupishly, you're letting it out. This can be thrilling, of course. We flirt with the power of that ancient monster at sports matches and at kitsch events like the Eurovision Song Contest. Its leash becomes longer and looser when it emerges in the form of political fights. We're often all too happy to believe the very worst about those bastards on the other side of the aisle, those Trumpists, those Remainers, those communists, that fascist scum. Becoming a small voice lost in a massed chorus against the evil other can be a pleasure that feels almost spiritual. We're reaching down to our deepest human essence when we lose ourselves like this. We're touching our original sin and allowing it to take us over.

But we rarely feel like sinners. Another truth that's apparent from decades of research in social psychology is the fact that the human brain is not to be wholly trusted. It is a storyteller, and the hero of the gripping neurological yarn that it constantly spins is you. Assuming you're not suffering from something like clinical depression, your hero-making brain is likely to be busy making you feel superior to many of those around, in all sorts of ways, whilst dividing the world into simplistic groups of 'goodies' and 'baddies'.

It's thought that one of the most powerful self-directed biases the human has is the one that tells us we're more morally worthy than we really are. No matter how badly we behave, we can always find a version of events to tell in which we're the hero. It's only villains in cartoons (and, arguably, psychopaths) who have the capacity to truly cackle with glee at how beastly they're being. The rest of us – the most of us – simply experience ourselves as being justified and righteous and fair or the victims of intolerable provocation. The power of this delusion can hardly be exaggerated. From domestic abusers to murderers to Nazis to communists to their modern, digital-forwards descendants, the standard human mindset is, 'I'm right.'

But that 'rightness' is just a story. And story – whether it's that of the self or that of narrative fiction – is always untrustworthy. In order to be comprehensible, books and films reduce the radical complexity of reality. Moral truths are straightforward and real, things that exist like wondrous jewels or handsome princes. The hero wins. The villain loses. Brains, too, simplify the impossible complexity of our environment and behaviour. One result of this is that we're often oriented towards an ideology, left or right – a tribal master-narrative that explains the world. When we're young, and we discover our ideology for the first time, it can feel like we've encountered revealed truth, as if our eyes have suddenly been opened. In fact, the opposite is true. Ideology blinds us. It allows us to see only half the real picture, at best.

But this isn't how it seems. In order to help justify our groupish unfairness, and keep alive our image of ourselves as a good moral actor, our brain will justify its own terrible urges – and will be brilliant at it. After all, who better to fool you – to know *exactly* what to say to beguile you into believing that your most incendiary and partisan instincts are morally justified – than your own mind? It will assign the opposing group purely selfish motives. It will hear their most powerful arguments in a particular mode of spiteful lawyerliness, seeking to misrepresent or discard what they have to say. It will use the most appalling transgressions of their very worst members as a brush to smear them all. It will take those individuals and erase their depth and diversity. It will turn them into outlines; morph their tribe into a herd of silhouettes. It will deny those silhouettes the empathy, humanity and patient understanding that it lavishes on its own. And, when it does all this, it will make us feel great, as if we're the hero of an exhilarating story. If you want to know how evil happens, know that it's in the moments that we're most under the monster's power that we're most convinced we're right. Tribal rage is to doubt what fire is to gas. They cannot coexist.

Every human group, especially those that have experienced some kind of pressure as a unit, will be capable of generating endless reasons why the 'others' are not even worth our contempt. That many of these reasons will be true (they are human, after all) doesn't mean it's not wise to start recognising when that old monster's leash is becoming dangerously loose. If we want to fight injustice, we should be on constant watch, making sure that it's the actual injustice that we're fighting, and not every person who happens to belong to the group to which its most conspicuous perpetrators belong.

And we should watch for the signs: the telltale footsteps that groups leave in the psychic environment when they're busy imagining themselves to be climbing above all the others. Groups make things sacred. These sacred items can be abstract patterns that are made from cloth and flown from high poles or cut or burned into the skin during initiation ceremonies; they can be hats or badges; they can be songs; they can be books or scrolls; they can be places; they can be dead heroes. They're all, in some way, tribal markers. Read the book, make the pilgrimage, fly the flag, display the martyr's image and you proudly project your tribal identity to the world.

Another thing that groups make sacred are ideas. And, especially in the twenty-first century, when we're arguably less likely to kill someone over their choice of hat or hero, it's in these sacred ideas that much of the danger lies. You can tell when an idea has become sacred to you, because you are irrationally emotional about it. If a person even threatens to question the validity of your sacred idea, you'll feel the lurching of that monstrous ape in your blood. For some people, gun ownership is a sacred idea. For some, it's women and womanhood. For some, its whiteness. For some, it's blackness. For some, it's free markets. For some, it's social justice. There aren't many of us who can honestly say we hold no ideas to be sacred. But when we boil with emotion at a tribal enemy who dares to even question them, we put ourselves in danger. In that moment, the very thing we're using to experience the world, and our place within it, is bending and distorting. The brain's inbuilt biases mean we have become morally untrustworthy, even to ourselves.

Nobody is innocent. Black, white, straight, gay, male, female, trans, if you own a human brain, you own that sin. Your nasty old ape – its deep, evolved neural embodiment – is always trying to shake free, and to fool you into believing in its virtue. And how tempting it is! Just as you possess ancient, evolved circuitry that cajoles you into gorging on chocolate or cheese, whispering into your ear, 'go on – after the day you've had, you know you deserve it', so powerful mechanisms coax you into being tribal. But it's a trap. And if you're a white person who says, 'what the blacks don't understand', you've fallen into it. If you're a black person who says, 'let me tell you about white people', you've fallen into it. If you're a man who says 'bloody women', you've fallen into it. If you're a woman who says, 'the problem with men is', you've fallen into it. If you're telling a person what they can say, what they can write, how they can dance or dress or wear their hair, on the basis of their gender, race, age, sexuality or social class, you've fallen into it. When you're in the grip of your original sin, you'll want to convince yourself you're the noble exception. That voice in your head will tell you, 'well, of course we should judge people as individuals, and not be prejudicial, but this situation is different'. Stand up to that voice. Don't listen to it. It is your monster speaking.

But what can we do about it? If the story the brain tells of its own life and self is narrow and biased, then the way to broaden its view seems obvious. We should feed into it stories of other people, nourishing it with new perspectives until it begins stretching at its edges. During the nineteenth century, slave narratives brought thousands of readers into the lives of those trapped in bondage in the Southern states of America. Books such as the *Narrative of the Life of Frederick Douglass* sold by the tens of thousands and gave abolitionists a fantastic weapon. The novel *One Day in the Life of Ivan Denisovich* by Aleksandr Solzhenitsyn dragged its readers through the experiences of an ordinary prisoner in one of Stalin's gulag camps, shocking the Soviet Union on its publication in 1962. The anti-war message of Erich Maria Remarque's *All Quiet on the Western Front* was felt to be so threatening to the Nazis that they set copies of it on fire. If tribalism is our original sin, then reading is like prayer. Original sin may be ineradicable, but story can help quieten its monster, turning its head and muffling its growl.

The Leavers of Boston

Edward Platt

The box of votes from the other polling station had arrived, and the women sitting at the table in front of the uncurtained window were sorting the folded papers into trays marked with the candidates' names. It was a cold February night, and the sense of the peat-black fields that lay unseen in the darkness made the lighted room seem even more welcoming – and the rituals of local politics even more vital. I was the first to arrive, but others soon followed, most of them in blue rosettes: the Tories were out 'mob-handed' to underscore the scale of their inevitable victory, Don Ransome said when he arrived to hear the result. Don was the UKIP candidate in the by-election in the ward of Old Leake and Wrangle, in the Fens north of Boston. It had been called when the long-standing Tory councillor had stepped down to look after her ailing husband. Don had spent the day at the dentist, having emergency surgery on a tooth, and he hadn't campaigned much before that, for he knew he wasn't going to win. He didn't seem concerned. 'When the political wind is against you, you just have to keep smiling,' he said.

He could afford to be magnanimous, for UKIP had recently

secured a victory in Boston that made defeat in a by-election seem trivial. The presence of the local Tory MP, Matt Warman – one of the many men and women in blue rosettes – confirmed the nature of the shift UKIP had helped to engineer. Warman had campaigned for Remain in the run-up to the June 2016 referendum about Britain's continued membership of the European Union, but afterwards he had switched sides, and taken up the Leavers' cause that UKIP had championed for so long. How a Remainer was chosen to represent Boston and Skegness is another question, for it was the most pro-Leave constituency in Britain. Very nearly three-quarters of votes (74.9 per cent) in Boston and Skegness were cast in favour of leaving the EU – the mirror image of Islington, the London borough where I live, where a fraction over 75 per cent of votes were in favour of the UK remaining a member.

Islington was so pro-Remain that, on the morning after the vote, I met a friend who had got to the polling station late, and seeing names uncrossed on the list, suggested that low turnout had contributed to the defeat. It didn't occur to her that those who hadn't voted might have voted Leave – they could only have been Remainers who stayed at home. The instinctive assumption that our neighbours were on our side went deeper than party loyalties, for the vote was more important than a party contest: we live with a general election result for five years at most, but we will feel the consequences of the EU referendum for at least a generation. And the arguments were so strongly felt they seemed to divide the country into two irreconcilable camps. Were you a member of the liberal metropolitan elite, a citizen of nowhere, cut off from the rest of Britain, yet still patronisingly intent on telling it how to live – or were you an insular, backward-looking xenophobe, preoccupied by the notion of reviving a vanished Britain that had probably never existed, irrespective of the cost to yourself?

The division existed on many levels, from the domestic to the geopolitical. It ran through families – and threatened to break up the United Kingdom, for Scotland and Northern Ireland voted one way and England and Wales the other. Within England, it deepened the divide between the capital and the regions. London isn't the only English city that voted Remain: many others, including Liverpool and Bristol – two places that I know and love – did as well. But London always styles itself as exceptional and, after the vote, there were suggestions that it should split from the rest of the country, and become a kind of city state within the EU – an island of Remain in a sea of Leave.

I disliked that idea as much as I disliked the idea of Britain leaving the European Union. I have lived in London for twenty-five years, but I still don't think of myself as a Londoner, and the unanimity of opinion in Islington in the weeks after the vote made me conscious of being cut off from the places where I grew up. I got so tired of meeting people at parties or at the school gates who claimed that Leavers had committed 'an act of self-harm', as if they were incapable of understanding the implications of their choice, that I started arguing their case. Perhaps Brexit wouldn't be as disastrous as people seemed to think. Perhaps it would work out well. Or perhaps it wouldn't make much difference in the end. That seemed easier to believe in the stunned aftermath of the vote when nothing changed but no one could talk about anything else.

Trolling my fellow Islingtonians had its limits. People were upset, and I understood why: I agreed with almost everything they said, and I only had to hear a Brexiteer on the radio – or see Michael Gove's name in print – to be reminded of the rage I had felt during the referendum debate. I still didn't understand why anyone might have voted Leave, let alone campaigned for it. I didn't understand the dislike of the EU or the idea that 'global Britain' will flourish when liberated from its constraints. That was why I found myself at the count in the Old Leake and Wrangle, witnessing the conclusion of Don Ransome's unsuccessful by-election campaign. Don and his wife Sue are the most devoted and prominent Leave campaigners in the most pro-Leave town in Britain, and I thought that if anyone could help me understand Brexit, it might be them.

Striking up a conversation across the divide that has come to dominate national debate proved harder than I had hoped. I had emailed the leader of UKIP in Boston, but we couldn't find a time to meet, and I got the impression that he would rather not. Don Ransome would be the best person, he said, for Don was always willing to help. We met for the first time in a pub in the centre of Boston, two weeks before the by-election. It was five o'clock: the pub was very quiet, although the red and yellow lights set up for the regular karaoke nights confirmed it wasn't always. There were three people at the bar – all Leavers, in a town of them – who joined in our conversation from time to time, throwing out praise for Nigel Farage and Jacob Rees-Mogg as if hoping to provoke the Remainer from London. They were friendly, and keen to make their case: one of them had been interviewed by the *New York Times* during the referendum, when Boston was identified as the epicentre of the anti-immigrant sentiment that was driving the vote for Leave. But most people in Boston were tired of the media, Don said: UKIP couldn't find anyone willing to be interviewed any more. Even Don's wife, Sue, was reluctant to speak to me. Don introduced us when they arrived at the count in Old Leake on the night of the by-election, and she struggled to be polite. 'This is Ed,' Don said. 'I guessed as much,' Sue said, and turned away. It was late, and she was tired, but even so, I was surprised by her rudeness. 'I've got nothing to say about the EU,' she said later; 'I just want to get out as soon as we can.' Her attitude made me even more appreciative of the patience and good humour that Don had shown.

He lost, as expected. He was beaten into third place by the Labour Party, which had never had much presence in the villages north of Boston, but he didn't regret standing. If he hadn't, the fifty people who voted for him would have been disenfranchised, he said, which showed admirable respect for the democratic process. Besides, it was useful to know their core vote in Old Leake and Wrangle. And third wasn't last: they had beaten a new party called Blue Revolution, which had been set up by a former Tory councillor who was sitting in the front row, with two of his colleagues. The three of them made up Blue Revolution in its entirety, as far as I could gather, but Don was respectful of them as well: their fledgling party reminded him of UKIP in its early days, 'when defeat was on repeat'. And its existence was in keeping with Boston's dissident tradition.

Boston used to be the second largest port in England, which exposed it to intellectual influence from the Continent, including the teachings of the radical Protestant reformer John Calvin. In the late fifteenth century, it became a centre of religious dissent, and a point of departure for those seeking religious freedom in other parts of the world. In 1607, a group of Separatist pilgrims from Nottingham boarded a boat near Boston in an attempt to escape to the Netherlands, where they hoped they would be free to worship as they chose. They were arrested, brought back to Boston, and tried in the Guildhall, but a year later they tried again: this time, they reached Leiden, and in 1620, they joined the party of pilgrims who sailed for the New World in the *Mayflower*.

Their departure did not diminish Boston's ardour for religious freedom. In 1612, a man called John Cotton became the vicar of St Botolph's, the imposing parish church known as the Stump, thanks to its lantern tower, which is visible for miles around in the flat landscape of the Fens. The memorial in the graveyard calls Cotton the 'First Teacher' of the Massachusetts Bay Colony, which was planned and financed nearby. Other memorials record the dates of local people who followed the pilgrim fathers to America, at Cotton's prompting – many left in 1630, and in the same year they established a city on the Shawmut Peninsula, which took the name of Cotton's home town, which in turn took its name from his church (St Botolph was a Saxon monk who supposedly founded a monastery near Boston in the seventh century, and over the years, Botolph's Town became Botulphstone, which became Boston).

Cotton had wanted to reform the Anglican Church from the inside, but in 1633 he sailed for America as well, and became the second pastor of Boston, Massachusetts. 'The lantern of St Botolph's ceased to burn, / When from the portals of that church he came, / To be a burning and a shining light, / Here in the wilderness,' run the lines by Longfellow inscribed on the memorial in the graveyard of the Stump. Yet over the years, the tidal river that flows past St Botolph's, and its memorials to the other Boston's founding fathers, has silted up, cutting off the town from the sea, and reducing its significance as a port. The outward migration has slowed as well: lately, the movement has been inwards, and the restlessness that played such an important role in the founding of the New World has found a different kind of expression.

Boston, Lincs occupies a blank spot in my mental map of England. I like to think I know most parts of the country, through personal experience or family connections. I was born in Essex and grew up in Northumberland, Merseyside, Hampshire and Bristol. Since my mother came from Norfolk and my father from Hull, I know parts of the east coast, as well – but not the middle section between the Wash and Lincoln. The Fens are blank in other ways, as well, or seem so to those who do not know them: before they were drained, outsiders regarded them as an unhealthy, featureless waste of dank pools and sodden meadows, and even now, our hold on them seems temporary and provisional. 'They are never reclaimed, only being reclaimed,' writes Graham Swift in *Waterland*, his great novel of Fenland life. And it is not just rainfall or storm surges, like the one of

December 2013 that flooded Boston, that threaten them, but the sea that has advanced and retreated through the gaps in the chalk barrier of the east coast several times in the last 10,000 years, laying down the bed of silt, clay and peat that makes the land so fertile.

If Kent is the garden of England, then the Fens are its allotment, I thought as I drove up to Boston on the night of the by-election. The embankments that carry the roads and rivers are like the trodden paths and railway sleepers that structure urban plots, and the red-brick houses standing among the clumps of trees are its sheds, built on the scale to match the seemingly endless fields. I passed the depots of farming companies, water treatment plants and household waste recycling centres. It was a bitter day, with a wind that warned of snow to come, as the weather system that would become known as the Beast from the East made landfall, but there were gangs of migrant workers in the fields, in long, snaking rows, stooped forward, picking cauliflowers or cabbages.

Local people used to do the back-breaking work on the land, and they would earn good money for it – as much as £500 a week each. 'You'd see them in the pubs on Friday night, getting paid,' Don said, by which he meant getting drunk. If more workers were needed, they used to bring them in by mini-buses from cities in the north and the Midlands. Then the EU 'opened the floodgates', Don said – and unlike other countries, Britain made no attempt to limit the number of migrants from the new member states.

According to the 2001 census, the biggest foreign community in Boston consisted of 249 Germans, and 98.5 per cent of Boston's population of 55,753 said they were white British. The Portuguese were the first to arrive, but they were soon replaced by the Eastern Europeans. When ten countries including Slovakia and the Czech Republic joined the EU in 2004, British prime minister Tony Blair said the UK would take 13,000 workers, but the total was exceeded in a month, Don claimed. By 2011, 10.6 per cent of the population of 64,600 – or 6,847 of 8,847 new arrivals – came from one of the new countries of the EU such as Poland, Lithuania, Latvia or Romania. That was seven years ago. Don estimated that one-third of Boston's population of 60,000 are now migrants. The landlord of the pub where we met the first time said there were forty-three foreign-owned shops. He had owned one himself, but he said he couldn't compete with the Eastern Europeans on price, for they sold cheap drink and cigarettes smuggled through the ports of the east coast. From time to time, trading standards officers carry out raids. But there are too many shops to cope with. There are illegal stills as well: five men were killed in 2011 when an illegal vodka distillery on an industrial estate blew up.

It was arguable that the presence of the Eastern Europeans was in keeping with the history of the town. In its heyday, Boston was a member of the Hanseatic League, the trading alliance composed of cities of the North Sea and the Baltic, yet as the River Witham silted up, its significance as a port declined. Unlike Liverpool, which never lost its connection with the sea or its outward-looking perspective, the town gradually forgot the connections with Eastern Europe that generated its medieval prosperity, and does not recognise that the migrants arrived on currents as natural as the ones that were propelling snow towards the east coast. Don did not accept the idea: 'The history of the town doesn't relate to where it is today,' he said, with a rare degree of impatience. 'What people see is lots of groups of men wandering around town. What they see is lots of very bad driving.'

The migrants were good workers, he acknowledged – and cheap, though many of them were exploited by 'their own people', in the form of gang-masters, who made them pay for transport, and to work. Yet British firms employed migrants as well. He mentioned one company that houses hundreds of Romanians in caravans in a camp in the marsh outside Old Leake: it pays them £3 an hour and justifies the wage by giving them English lessons and saying they are students. I saw the camp on the night of the by-election, when I drove through Wrangle on the raised roads that wind across the empty fields, but I hadn't been inside: I emailed the CEO, asking if I could visit, but he refused politely. The subject of migrant workers provokes 'strong reactions, for and against', he said, though I was having trouble finding anyone prepared to make the case 'for'.

Don did not know any Eastern Europeans, and none of the people I approached in the street or in shops would speak to me. It was evidence of the suspicions in the town, Don said. 'Unfortunately, a lot of people are resentful of what they refer to as the foreigners: there's no integration between the locals and the Eastern Europeans.' The causes of the divide were not primarily economic. It was true that the locals were unable to compete on price, but they had adapted by becoming electricians or building contractors. Unemployment was low. The sense of being excluded from the country's prosperity may have driven the Brexit vote in other parts of the country, but Boston is booming. Its problem is not dereliction but overcrowding. Many of the migrants live in HMOs, or Houses in Multiple Occupation – terraced houses converted into dorms, with bunk beds in every room. Even the ground floors, which are meant to be kept empty in case the Haven bursts its banks again, as it did in 2013, were lived in. And people have spilled out of the houses as well: they are living in caravans beside the Haven and in tents on the path that runs to the boundary of the port. Others live in garages on the edge of town or sleep in greenhouses in the Fens, even in the middle of winter.

Even in the daytime, the streets are crowded, for people can't stay at home: there is nowhere to sit or watch TV in the HMOs, and they are not allowed to smoke or drink inside. I spent most of a day wandering around the streets of Boston, and I was not alone: all day, I passed people who were doing the same. The town seemed calm enough, but Don said it wasn't calm at night, when the fights were often on ethnic lines. 'The Russians can't stand the Poles,' Don said. 'The Bulgarians don't like the Romanians. Boston used to be a sleepy market town – there was the usual punch-up on a Saturday night. But now we're seeing stabbings – we've become the murder capital of Britain. We have a higher murder rate than London. It has changed completely. The level of violence has escalated. You would be hard-pushed to find someone who says they feel safe in Boston at night. And I know women who say they do not feel safe in the day.'

Taxi drivers keep their doors locked, for people would get into the cabs and start fighting. The police didn't have the manpower to cover it. The police station, which stands on the banks of the Haven, was like the *Marie Celeste*. 'There just aren't enough police officers in Lincolnshire,' Don said. I wondered at his account of a town descending into ethnic strife. Most English county towns are raucous at night, and a policeman that I spoke to at the count agreed that Boston was hardly exceptional. There was trouble, he acknowledged, but it was rarely on national lines. If someone felt like a fight, they didn't care who it was with. Besides, it was nothing new: it was the same back in the 1940s, when the locals fought the RAF crews who were stationed in the Fens.

It didn't matter where the new arrivals came from, Don and Sue said, repeatedly: after all, neither of them were from Boston. When Sue moved up from Leighton Buzzard, thirty years ago, she was met with suspicion, for the locals were tired of southerners looking for cheap housing. Don was from Huntingdon. 'I was always interested in the services,' he told me, the first time we met. As a child, he desperately wanted to be a soldier and, at the age of nineteen, he joined the Royal Air Force. 'I was working in a sawmill and I thought there must be a better life. And I never looked back.' He was wearing a shirt with the logo of the Air Training Corps, for he was heading for a meeting later in the evening: he had started in the ATC and he was still working with it, more than forty years later. His last full-time posting was at RAF Coningsby, and when he left the Air Force in 1989, after twelve years, he started an airport transfer business. Sue, who was from Luton, had moved to Lincolnshire to be near her parents, and she was also working as a taxi driver. They met in the taxi rank.

Don's involvement with UKIP began in 1999, after a 'road to Damascus' moment: he had always voted Conservative and he had always been anti-EU, and one day a colleague coming back from holiday gave him a leaflet to read. It was everything he believed in. Two weeks later, a group of Boston fishermen invited Nigel Farage and Jeffrey Titford, then MEP for the East of England and Farage's predecessor as UKIP leader, to address a meeting in Boston. Two weeks after that, the town's first UKIP branch was formed. Don, who is now sixty, balding and stooped, was a founding member – 'the only one still going'.

Sue resisted getting involved for a long time. Her upbringing had inoculated her against political commitment, she said, when we met the morning after the by-election, for her mother was a secretary to a Labour MP in South Bedfordshire, and her father was a communist. 'He was as red as you could go,' Don said, though despite their differing views, he and his father-in-law got on 'like a house on fire'. As a teenager, Sue joined the Labour Party and then the Liberals, and canvassed for a local Liberal politician called Steve Owens, but by the time she moved to Boston, she had had enough: she didn't even want politics discussed in the house. Then she heard Nigel Farage on the radio one day, and she said to Don, 'I like this bloke: is he in your party? Is he as good-looking as he sounds?' He got out a videotape and she joined UKIP that evening.

Don stood in a by-election for the first time in 2003, and in 2008 he was elected to the parish council. Yet he never became a member of the county or borough council, despite standing many times. Sue was more successful: she was elected to the parish council in 2008, the county council in 2009 and the borough council in 2011. And their daughters followed suit. As soon as they were old enough to stand, they put their names forward, and in 2013, two of them were elected to 'County' as well, borne on the surge of popularity that propelled UKIP to a role of national and international significance. 'We were a little bit ahead of the rest of the country, but that was Boston for you,' Sue said. It was also the Ransomes. Sue gave an interview for ITN in St Botolph's on the night of the referendum shortly before Nigel Farage conceded defeat, but by the time she and Don got home, the result had been reversed. Sue said she was going to ring Farage. Don said he wouldn't answer, but he picked up straightaway. 'Did you see the vote in Boston?' Sue said, and he said, yes – and it's all thanks to you and Don. Sue was pleased – 'I thought, well, now we have arrived' – and you couldn't blame her: they had won in Boston, and UKIP had won in the country as a whole, for there would not have been a referendum if it hadn't been for its success in attracting Tory Eurosceptics. Perhaps it was inevitable that it hadn't been able to sustain such heights. But the Ransomes' support hadn't wavered: Don said UKIP had lost a few thousand 'fair-weather friends', but nothing more, and Sue was so intent on affirming her loyalty to the cause that she had painted her nails in the party colours of purple and gold. Even the pub where she had suggested we meet contained a political message: it was a Wetherspoons, the chain owned by the Brexiteer Tim Martin, and there were beermats promoting an organisation called 'Fishing for Leave' on the tables and the bar. 'People say it's over,' Sue said. 'I say, "Well it might be over for you: it's not over for me."'

She was far more amenable than she had been the night before, though she was still very forthright, and made a point of saying so. 'I speak as I find,' she said more than once, as if acknowledging a propensity to give offence might lessen its effects – or allow her to continue to indulge it. I didn't mind, for I was curious to know how her views had formed. She saw her career as a continuation and rejection of her background. Her political commitment was 'the old family stuff coming out', she said, though she had not taken up her parents' cause, and she also traced her antipathy to the EU to her background. She remembered going to the supermarket in Leighton Buzzard, where she used to live, and being dismayed that she couldn't get Australian cheddar or New Zealand apples. The idea that we were betraying our friends in the Commonwealth by taking up with our European neighbours had been aired in the referendum campaign of 1975, when we voted to join the EU, though in hindsight, it doesn't make sense to me: why would anyone – and particularly a professed patriot – want cheddar and apples from the other side of the world when we produce our own?

Sue must have recognised how weak the argument sounded, for she said that she had been influenced by her parents' concern for value for money. Yet she didn't need to explain. I didn't understand, but I didn't expect to, for we had reached the part of the argument that defies rational explication. Leavers believe that the EU threatens the British way of life, and Remainers don't. I asked for examples of Brussels' nanny-statism, which Sue had complained of, and as usual they seemed unconvincing, if not made up: had Brussels really issued laws about the directions swings could face? Sue thought it had. I couldn't dispute her claim that one of her children came home from school with a diary that contained dates from European history, instead of British, but I can say that nothing like that has ever happened to me. My children go to state schools and they have never come home with anything resembling EU propaganda.

Naturally, Sue wanted the old emblems of British identity restored: she wanted her old blue passport back and she wanted to see the Union Jack on her driving licence. I understood that, to the extent that I like having a European passport, though I would have given it up it if I had to, for it is only a bureaucratic symbol. After the referendum, I wished the EU had placated the burgeoning nationalism in its member states by restoring a few harmless emblems of patriotic pride, and I accepted the Leavers' case that its self-aggrandising bureaucracy would not permit it. It wasn't until several months later that it became apparent that the burgundy passports had never been mandatory at all: Sue could have had her blue passport back at any time.

Yet it wasn't only Britain that had suffered from the EU's empire-building. 'I don't want other countries to lose their identity, either,' she said – though she didn't explain why she thought they might. It is not a new concern: I remember arguing about the agglomerating effects of the EU with a friend of a friend as along ago as 1992, after I had moved to London from Paris, where I had been living. John Major was forcing the Maastricht Treaty through the House of Commons in the face of opposition from the nascent Eurosceptic movement, and the person I was talking to took the soon-to-be-familiar view that the process would mould the countries of Europe into a single ball, like a lump of plasticine, turning its bright colours muddy brown.

I didn't believe it then and, twenty-six years later, I still don't. I wondered why the people who attach most significance to national culture are also most concerned by its fragility: they might say they fear its loss more intensely. But I believe that national identity is more robust than they seem to think. And I don't think membership of the EU is incompatible with patriotic pride: I am English, but I am also British and European, and I don't regard those identities as incompatible. In fact, I believe they are mutually enriching and socially beneficial: it is when we begin defining people with a single, simplistic label such as Jew or Catholic – or Remainer or Leaver – that we make it harder to see the things we have in common, and create the conditions in which prejudice, and worse, violence and intimidation, are allowed to flourish. I didn't believe the Ransomes were guilty of such ugly feelings, and I knew that millions of people shared their concerns about the loss of national identity. I felt no closer to understanding them. In that respect, I felt I had learned nothing from my trips to Boston. Yet I had begun to get a better sense of the circumstances in Boston that had persuaded the Ransomes, and so many others, to take up the Leavers' cause. I had also begun to see how the town might transcend them.

Don and I agreed on several things – that the referendum campaign had been a bad-tempered, uninformative debate that had probably not changed anyone's mind; that the result was, nonetheless, irreversible; and that Brexit would not be as revolutionary as its proponents seemed to think. Change would be slow and gradual: we agreed on that – though we disagreed on its effects. I believe we will expend unquantifiable reserves of political, bureaucratic and diplomatic energy demolishing our relationship with Europe, only to have to reconstruct it on less advantageous terms, leaving us poorer, culturally and materially, while the Ransomes believe we will benefit hugely by regaining control of immigration – though even in that respect, change will be less dramatic than some people hope. 'We're not trying to pull up the drawbridge,' Don said. The people who thought the migrants would all be dumped on barges and shipped off to Dover were not UKIP supporters, he said – or at least, not ones they had ever met. Every country needs immigration, he acknowledged, 'but it has to be people that we want and need – not people who want and need to be here.'

I doubted that the process could be managed as adeptly as he seemed to think, but I didn't doubt that it could be managed better than it had been in Boston. In November 2017, the town got a grant of £1.39 million to 'promote community cohesion' and help it adapt to the effects of so many new arrivals; had it got it ten years ago, things might have been different, the Ransomes said. Yet even their despairing portrait of life in the town contained suggestions that Boston was beginning to reach a new accommodation. Even Don recognised that some of the migrants were part of the new generation the country needed, for they were well educated and ambitious: 'They won't follow their parents onto the land,' he said: 'They won't be out there in minus five degrees, cutting cauliflowers. They will be CEOs, lawyers, doctors.'

Some would move on to places that offered greater opportunities than Boston. Others would settle down and renew the town in different ways, for ethnic differences or economic disparities never stop people falling in love or getting married. Relationships between Polish girls and English boys were the most common, which seems true in London as well. And there were friendships forming, too, some very close to home: the Ransomes' son – who was the only member of the family never to have stood for UKIP – knew Latvians and Lithuanians. Some of them had helped Sue and Don around the house when Don was 'poorly'. One of them was helping move a cupboard one day when he asked Sue if she wanted to kick them out if they won the referendum. She reassured him that they didn't. 'I said, "No way, you are here – you stay here." And he said, "Good: well, if you win, will you send the rubbish home?"'

I didn't like the word 'rubbish': Don had used it once, and I hadn't liked it then, either. Like their claim that the argument was about 'space not race', it struck an uncharacteristically harsh note. Their evident delight that a migrant had used the same term made me uncomfortable as well, for they seemed to regard it as confirmation of concerns that they would rather not voice: you see, they were implying, it isn't just us who don't like them. And yet it was possible to see even this questionable anecdote as evidence that awareness of the complexity of the migration was growing: it confirmed that the new arrivals were not a monolithic group, but a collection of individuals who made unflattering distinctions amongst themselves – and that, in turn, made me think that the pattern of resistance that always accompanies the movement of people was reaching an accommodation that would endure long after the arguments about membership of a political alliance had faded.

abutment

Gillian Allnutt

but for the askance in her
but for the biding in abeyance of her
but for the clairvoyance that came to her like a grandmother
but for the expanse of love in her the lark in the clear air
but for the auld acquaintedness with violence in her

*'Gillian has always been difficult' my parents used to say, apologetically. Here she is
in all her awkwardness: the wretched little stranger in myself: my self. She's taught
me more about how to be human than anyone else I know.*

Fast as Lightning

Peter Ho Davies
from *The Fortunes*

Soon it'll be three decades. A ceremony is planned, a memorial. A plaque to be unveiled. It's more than a year away yet, but I already have an invitation. To attend, to say a few words, to share my recollections. It lies on my desk. *Never forget*, it says. *Always remember. Keep his memory alive.*

At the bottom in smaller font it also says, *Save the day*. A typo, though I must have read it three times before I even noticed. Now it's all I can think of, that malapropism. Maybe it's why I've not written back yet to decline, as I've declined all such invitations for years. It's a mistake my father might easily have made, anyone of his immigrant generation. I wonder if the letter writer is older, or more likely someone still hearing an elder's voice in his head.

What do I remember? What does anyone remember after all this time?

If you remember it at all, if you were around in the eighties, say, what you remember is a Chinese guy being beaten to death in Detroit by two white auto-workers who mistook him for a Japanese.

This at the height of the import scare, when Japanese manufacturers were being blamed for the collapse of the Big Three US auto companies.

Maybe you remember it happened outside a club where the Chinese guy – actually a Chinese-American, name of Vincent Chin – was celebrating his bachelor party. Maybe you remember he was buried on what should have been his wedding day.

But perhaps you thought it was just an urban legend, a bad joke come to life.

Chinaman and a Jew walk into a bar, order drinks. They get to chatting, then out of nowhere the Jew turns round and sucker punches the Chinaman in the face.

'What the hell was that for?' splutters the Chinaman, and the Jew goes: 'Pearl Harbor.'

'But that was the Japanese, I'm Chinese!'

'Oi! Sorry. You've all got the black hair, and slanty eyes. It was an honest mistake.'

(Stop me if you've heard this one before.)

'Well all right,' Chinaman says and they shake and order another round.

But ten minutes later, the Chinaman rears back, cold cocks the Jew.

'What the hell was that for?' the Jew asks, picking himself up.

'The Titanic,*' Chinaman says.*

'The Titanic?*' the Jew cries. 'The* Titanic! *That was a fucking iceberg.'*

'Iceberg, Goldberg, Steinberg,' the Chinaman says. 'Honest mistake!'

Only that night it wasn't a Chinaman and a Jew, it was two

Chinamen, Vincent and me. And it wasn't a bar, but a strip club. And we were with a couple of white friends, Bill and Jerry. But still.

I don't know about an honest mistake, but it was an easy one. It was dark in there, filmed with smoke, lit only by the snowy static of glitter balls. One of the girls used a fog machine in her routine, another flickered in a strobe. I'm not sure *I* could have told Chinese from Japanese in that light. But I knew the pair – one silvering, the other mustachioed – across the stage were white. And they knew we weren't.

He wasn't a saint, Vincent, though he always figured he might have been named for one. The newspapers all reported he was there for his bachelor party, and sure that was the occasion, but 'bachelor party' makes it sound like a one-off, like *we* took *him* there, when it was his idea, and a regular haunt of his, his *turf*. The Fancy Pants lounge in Highland Park. The girls all knew him, he was a favourite. Contrary to the stereotype – which is why I say it – he wasn't a eunuch.

The only thing that was different about that night, then? It was supposed to be his last time. He told me his mother had given him the ultimatum (*she* knew about the club, his mom, though not his fiancée Vicki, for her it was almost as shocking as his death). He'd promised he'd quit going after he married. *It's the last time, Ma.* I remember because he said she didn't like that, him saying *last time*. She was superstitious that way, said it was bad luck. 'Can't win,' is what he shouted over the music, his breath warm in my ear. Me, I didn't believe him anyway, figured he'd be back the week after the honeymoon.

Maybe I even hoped so secretly. It was the first time he'd asked me since I moved home after college, my first time ever in a strip club. I'd dressed preppy – pastel polo, over khakis and topsiders. Jerry in his mullet and acid-washed jeans laughed when I got in the car.

'It's not a disco, man! The girls dance for you, not *with* you.'

'Ah, lay off him.'

I was working towards my CPA back then; Vincent had come straight from the restaurant, still in his black slacks, and white shirt, but he'd slipped on his Members Only jacket. He was riding shotgun and from the backseat I watched him spread the wings of his collar in the visor mirror to reveal a thin gold chain.

The papers also said what a filial son he was, working two jobs – draftsman by day, waiter by night – to support his poor widowed mother, as well as save for his wedding. They made him out to be a model citizen of the model minority. Saint *and* stereotype. But think. That night he must have had fifty bucks in smoothed out singles on him – 'Tips, baby!' – so what exactly was he working so hard for? Two jobs to pay for two lives, maybe.

So, no saint.

Our generation's Bruce Lee, someone once called him. Meaning our generation's tragic martyr. Such an American concept (see Lincoln, Abe; Kennedys, assorted; Doctor King; not to mention James Dean, Marilyn Monroe). But Bruce Lee, for all that he was born in the US, always felt more Chinese than Chinese-American, and at least as popular with whites and blacks. Plus, his

74

death – an allergic reaction to medication – lacked a bad guy (one reason rumours of triad plots, or drug abuse – shades of those old Chinatown evils – abounded).

But now we had our own martyr.

I always wondered how I was supposed to feel about that. I was the friend, after all. Could I have saved him? Should I have died with him? But then he wouldn't be a martyr, or perhaps we both would be (though martyrs – like most symbols – come best in ones). Instead, I was the witness. In all the newspaper accounts, and now online if you care to look it up, 'his friend who ran away'.

If you can be a friend, and run away.

Without Bruce Lee, though, would two white men have brought a baseball bat to a fight with an Asian? Had they seen his movies? Did they think they were only being smart, evening the odds against some kung fu fighter? Vincent did look a little like Bruce – that same thick mop of coal-black hair. So did I, for that matter. We didn't look alike, but we looked like Bruce, more like him than each other probably. We'd spent our teens practising his sprung stride, and sudden, panting punches, flashing his switchblade smile in the mirror.

Horse walks into a bar – you know this one? – *and the bartender asks, 'Why the long face?'*

Yeah? How about this one?

Two Chinamen walk into a bar and the barkeep goes, 'Why the same face?'

*

OK. But we weren't the same. That's my point. *That's* what got him killed.

On the one hand he was more Chinese than me, and most of the other Chinese-American kids I knew. He was born there, lived there until he was six before he was adopted (itself pretty rare back then), didn't even speak English in first grade. Then again his parents didn't live in or around Chinatown like most of ours. They were in Highland Park, with no Chinese neighbors. Oh, they came to Chinatown to do their shopping every weekend – I'd see him around, knew who he was – but Highland Park was where he lived, where he went to school. With white kids. Poles, Irish, Italian. (This was before the riots, white flight.) So he was always more at ease with them, more at ease with them than we were, for sure, but also maybe more at ease with them than with *us*. That's where he met Bill and Jerry, in grade school. I only knew him well in high school; they always had that first claim on him.

It's one reason Vincent liked the Fancy Pants, even though it was a rat hole – an old grindhouse with rows of movie seats still in back, and the girls up on stage, beneath the peeling gilt proscenium. It meant he got to go back to Highland Park, back home. He'd always hated having to leave. *Driven out*, as he saw it. His dad had been mugged, so they'd moved to the suburbs and Vincent had finished high school there. They traded a third-floor walk-up for a nice little ranch with a car port and scalloped aluminum awnings two blocks over from ours.

My father talked about Oak Park like it was the promised land. But it never sat right with Vincent. 'Can't sleep right,' he complained; he missed the *shush* of traffic at night. Really, it felt like running away, I think. He didn't blame his dad – Mr Chin was an older guy, in his sixties by then – but Vincent always figured he'd have fought back if it were him. You could say he'd been spoiling for that fight for years.

Irony is, he was a great runner. That was his thing in high school – track. I was heavy as a kid, shy in the cafeteria, so I'd take my lunch on the bleachers, watch him doing his laps. I told him running suited his name and he looked at me blankly. *Vincent*, I said, *means winner.* He liked that, as I hoped he would, but it surprised me he hadn't known. Then again he went by Vince, at school at least, itself unusual among us. Our boys' names, even in English, often echoing the two syllables of a Chinese name: Roland or Robin, Henry or Melvin, Eddie or Albert. Myself, I used to call him *InVince*, because he was invincible, I told him, but also because he was 'in' – in a way I never could be. Really I knew 'Vince' just meant American.

On the wedding invitation it was 'Vincent' in embossed italics. Vincent and Victoria. Both winners. Vicki and Vince. As a couple they couldn't have sounded more all-American. They were planning two ceremonies, Vicki had two dresses picked out, one Chinese, one Western. When I asked him that night how the planning was going, he told me his mother was arguing with Vicki over guests throwing rice. 'She says Chinese don't waste food, still remembers going hungry during the war.' The wedding was planned for a Monday when all the Chinese restaurants were closed so that everyone could attend. Afterwards, they had tickets for Aruba.

His middle name was Jen, though I only learned it when he died. He never used it and it only shows as J. on his gravestone. I had to ask what it stood for. Jen – the great Confucian virtue of doing unto others as you'd have them do unto you.

What do I remember? What do you?

If you remember the case at all, if you're Asian-American, say, you might recall that the killers, Evans and Pitts, father and stepson, pled manslaughter. It was just a bar-room brawl gone wrong, heat of the moment stuff – an honest mistake! – never mind it took them thirty minutes to hunt Vincent down. The victim had thrown the first punch, after all. They got off with probation, and fines of $3,000 each.

Less than the price of a used car, people said.

Maybe you remember that the judge had been in a Japanese POW camp during the war.

Remember when Chinese couldn't testify against whites, people said, as if it were yesterday and not a hundred years ago.

It was Vincent's idea. He told me to run. Only he didn't say 'run'. He said, 'Scram'. It was the last word I heard from him in English, so I've given it a lot of thought. Scram. It's what you say to a kid, isn't it? A nuisance. Or maybe what naughty kids say to each other, after they ring a doorbell. Scram. Not run. *He* was a runner. Running to him meant winning. Running *towards* something. Scram, I think, meant running away. If he'd said 'run' we might have both run, but 'scram' was for me. Because *he* didn't scram.

He waited for them. He could have gotten away. When Evans hopped out of the car – a Plymouth, for the record – it was still moving. It ran over his foot, for God's sake! It was the Keystone Klan out there! You think Vincent couldn't have outrun these guys? He lettered in track. But he was done running. He started it at the club after all. He would have fought in the gravel and dog-shit parking lot outside too if Evans hadn't gone for the bat. He *wanted* to fight them. Maybe he thought he could make Evans drop the bat, shame him into a fair fight. Maybe he figured just two-on-one they wouldn't feel they needed the bat.

This was on Woodward, by the McDonald's there.

I didn't run far. To the edge of the light. Just far enough to live, just far enough to watch.

Scram! Who was he to tell me to scram? Who was I to listen?

He was grappling with Pitts when Evans caught him on the knees, as if reaching for a grounder, after which Vincent couldn't have run even if he'd wanted. Then a line drive to the chest as he went down, two more to the head when he was on all fours. Swinging for the fences.

I did run back, but too late.

Vincent's last words – 'It's not fair' – to me, in Chinese, while I cradled his ruined head, blood bubbling from his mouth and nose as he spoke, blood pouring from his ears like oil. His skull felt like rotten fruit.

The blow to the chest broke a jade charm Vincent wore on his chain – a bad omen to Chinese, though you hardly needed an omen to foretell what was coming next.

The ambulance took him to Henry Ford Hospital (the same hospital he used to take his dad for dialysis) where he lingered for a few days, his mother by his bedside, calling him – 'Vincent! Mama coming. Vincent!' – as if from a great distance, before she finally gave consent to turn him off. The same hospital where they told her thirty years earlier that she'd never have a child.

If you remember the case at all (and maybe it's coming back to you?), if you were watching TV back then, you might recall her, Vincent's mother – Lily – going on *Donahue* (remember him?), or meeting with Jesse Jackson (remember *him?*) at one of his presidential campaign rallies. She put the yellow in the Rainbow Coalition, people said.

She still had one of those comedy Chinglish accents – *What I live for? I don't have happy anymore. I not care my life.* The kind of accent that makes my generation cringe; Vincent used to do a choice imitation of it. But her voice cracked, daring anyone to laugh, daring anyone to feel embarrassed. *Vely hurt my heart.*

Lily. But Mrs Chin to me, always. Just another mom, but stouter, shriller, fiercer and more doting than all the rest so that she seemed somehow like everyone's mother. (Everyone *else's*; mine had died of ovarian cancer before I turned seven.) When we were kids she always had treats – egg tarts, moon cakes in fall, her home-made prawn crackers – and she praised my appetite. When we grew up she was always asking when I was going to get married, telling Vincent to introduce me to some nice girl (to which he would roll his eyes, though whether for my benefit or hers, I was never quite sure).

All I learned about her life came from the papers. Some of it I doubt even Vincent knew. She'd grown up in Canton. Her family owned a department store. They must have been well off, but they lost it all in the war. She'd come from China in '47 to marry his dad who'd lived here since the twenties and earned his citizenship by enlisting. Mrs Chin's own father had resisted the match – an ancestor had worked on the railroads and been driven out – but she was sure it would be a better life. She'd seen so much violence in China at the hands of the Japanese she wanted to start over. She'd have been twenty-seven – old to marry, delayed by the war – and Vincent's dad even older at forty-four. I guess they tried to start a family of their own, but she miscarried and the docs told her she couldn't have kids. It took them more than a decade to adopt Vincent from Hong Kong. His dad was in his late fifties, by then, and even Lily in her forties – the oldest parents of anyone I knew.

They worked their whole lives in laundries and restaurants. 'For what?' Vincent asked me savagely during his father's final illness. 'They never had any fun.' We were outside in his drive, smoking, Mrs Chin framed in the kitchen window intently washing rice as if panning for gold. I knew what it was to lose a parent; I'd come to pay my respects. I didn't know his father well – what I remember most is his sure-handed ability to pluck out a fish's eyeball with his chopsticks, a deftness which impressed me as a child almost as much as his relish in eating it appalled me – but I knew the answer to Vincent's question. For what? *For you!* It was the same for all of us kids. The debt he could never redeem, no matter how late he sat up rubbing the old man's swollen knuckles when he couldn't sleep.

First his dad, now Vincent himself. Part of what was so moving was that his mother's desire for justice, her thirst for vengeance, they were ways of forgiving his most unfilial act: dying before her (beside which sneaking off to strip clubs under Vicki's nose was a pale betrayal). The night it happened, when I finally got home from the hospital and told my father everything he pulled me close and hugged me. I couldn't remember the last time we'd touched. I had failed my friend, I understood, but been a good son.

They called themselves the ACJ, American Citizens for Justice – no mention of Chinese or Asian in the name – and insisted that placards at marches be in English, which may explain the painful, plaintive pun of 'Chin Up for Justice' on one popular sign. But they're the ones – journalists, lawyers, church leaders and local businessmen – who helped Lily get the case reopened. And their coming together – Chinese and Japanese, those old enemies, as well as Korean, Vietnamese, Filipino – marked the start of a Pan-Asian political movement. And me along with the rest, attending meetings, giving interviews, marching beneath a neatly lettered sign. You could say it's when we became Asian-American. Two drunk white guys couldn't tell us apart, and we realised we were more alike than we'd thought.

The first meetings were held in the Golden Star, the restaurant where Vincent worked, everyone sitting around the fresh laid tables – plastic tablecloths and melamine rice bowls – trying not to disturb the settings, looking less angry or sad in that context than hungry. It reminded me of his funeral the previous summer, only these weren't all the same people who'd come then. I didn't know many of them;

many of them didn't know Vincent, and yet they spoke of that night as if they'd been there, as if *they'd* been attacked. In a way, I guess, they felt they had, if not by Evans, then by the verdict.

Part of me wanted to say something – *didn't they know who I was?* – but then it came to me that all their talk of a 'heinous assault', a 'brutal slaying' *wasn't* the way you'd talk about it if you were there. That wasn't how I remembered it, it was how they *imagined* it. They weren't talking as if they'd been there, but as if they *wished* they had been. What would they have done if they had? I wondered, and held my peace. It reminded me of Vincent, the way he told me about his father's mugging. They were spoiling for a fight too.

Back in the kitchen, I remember, the cooks were preparing dishes for later, hot oil singing in the steel woks.

I didn't say anything in the end, but Lily was there and she spoke last, halting but firm. She wanted justice for Vincent, and we applauded until our hands stung. But a lot of the people in that room also wanted justice for themselves. Me too, I suppose. I had failed my friend but maybe there was still something I could do.

Don't make a federal case out of it. Wasn't that the Chinese-American way? Turn the other cheek, look the other way, water off a Peking duck's back. 'Take it on the chin,' as a sick joke doing the rounds had it.

But making a federal case is literally what we did. What we had to do to get the case reopened and prosecuted by the Justice Department as a hate crime. Only it had never been done before. Civil Rights legislation hadn't been applied to Asians previously, doing so now was a hot topic, a *choice*. Whose lot to throw in with? Blacks, for whom the legislation had been written, some of whom were suspicious of a possible usurpation, or dilution, as if Asian struggles were equivalent? Or whites, whom many of us aspired to be like?

I sat at the back of those meetings, between the payphone and the cigarette machine. Every so often the talk would be interrupted, hushed really, by someone trying to come in to eat, the irritated exchanges at the door when they were turned away. I couldn't see from where I was, but I imagined they were probably white. It was that kind of restaurant, the kind where white diners point out the few Chinese to each other and whisper how the food must be 'authentic'. I wondered what they thought if they glimpsed a crowd of Chinese inside before the door shut on them.

As to our question: were we a minority or were we honorary members of the majority? I reckon I know what Vincent would have chosen. Vince. But to get justice for him, we choose the other. Later, I heard some blacks call us 'Fleedom Riders'.

So a federal case, and I was called to testify, to say what I'd heard, what I'd seen, what I'd done. What I remembered.

It *was* a race thing. No doubt. One of the strippers, Lacey, remembered the line, and then we all did. 'It's because of you little motherfuckers we're out of work,' Evans said, meaning Japanese, even though he wasn't out of work, himself, even though Vincent wasn't Japanese.

But OK, the car business *was* in the crapper, as Vincent very well knew. He was working for an auto-supplier, after all. He was *in* the business.

Would it have made a difference if Vincent had said *I'm Chinese*? That his mother had moved to the US because she couldn't live in China after the war, with her memories of the Japanese bombing? Probably not. Nips, Chinks, Gooks, Slants – we were all the same to them. Instead, he said 'I'm not a little motherfucker,' and Evans came back with drunken magnanimity: 'Big fucker, little fucker, we're all fuckers.' And then Vincent stubbed out his cigarette and went for him. Punches were thrown, a stool. Pitts had his head cut open.

I'm not a motherfucker, he said. And he wasn't. But it's the word that set him off, I think. More than the race thing, even. *That* we heard every day anyhow. But he didn't like *motherfucker*. He was an adoptee, his father had died less than a year earlier, he still lived at home, and he was about to get married. He didn't like that word. It's unfilial, OK. Disrespectful. We worship our ancestors.

I wonder sometimes about the odd echoes – an adoptee and his mother, a father and a step-son. Perhaps they all had something to prove. Evans did say, 'I was just defending my boy.' He was a superintendent at Chrysler when Pitts had been laid off, maybe he felt he owed him. Maybe he loved him like his own. They still *played* baseball together is why they had the bat in the trunk in the first place. Turns out Evans only took Pitts to the club that night because the boy had just had a fight with his girlfriend. And the day after (the only day either of them ever woke up in a cell)? Father's Day.

Vincent was my friend. So how could I leave him? He *was* my friend, but I didn't always like him. How could I not envy his confidence, his good looks, his fiancée? Even afterwards, I hated him a little. Even in death he made me feel like nothing, worse than nothing. A coward. Oh, it wasn't right, those two getting off for killing him. But that's not why I testified. I wanted to stand up, even if belatedly. *I* felt like the guilty party. So I met with Tina, the young Chinese lawyer, and Jerry and Bill, around a cigarette-burned table, and she told us, 'You need to get your lines down, agree on what happened, get your stories straight.' Tina was slim and a little severe, but her long hair shone like Vicki's. Vincent would have called her *fine*, found a way to make her smile. That's when we remembered the racist talk, heard by all of us above the throbbing music, clearly recalled despite all the booze we'd drunk.

And Vincent's last words? Heard only by me, spoken in Chinese so no one else could understand, never mind that his head was already stove in, jaw shattered and people wonder how he could even have retained consciousness, let alone spoken? Well, OK, but it *wasn't* fair, was it? None of it. Tell me that's not true.

What did I do? What would you have done?

Evans got twenty-five years.

Out the courtroom window, I watched a jet slowly raise a scar across the sky.

What is truth anyway? What I testified? This version? What you can read in the papers, or online? Chinese whispers, you might say.

Vincent, incidentally, wanted to be a lawyer when he was a kid; his mother told him no one would believe a Chinese lawyer. He wanted to be a writer too, but she told him he'd never make any money at it. By the time I knew him he was thinking about being a vet, but she reminded him he was scared of blood.

He *was* my friend. But did I like him, or was I just like him?

Maybe, just maybe, if you remember the case at all, if you saw the Oscar-nominated documentary, or studied it in school, or read a blog about it, you'll recall that Evans' federal conviction was later appealed.

Lacey's testimony was called into doubt. Had she received consideration for other charges?

And the witnesses' testimony – *our* testimony, our *memory* (by this time five years had passed since that night) – was challenged. We'd been coached by our Chinese lawyer, they said.

What did I remember? When did I remember it? I don't know. The air conditioning was blasting in court but my shirt was sticking to me like a Band-Aid. What if I didn't *want* to remember that night? Did anyone think of that?

Maybe you remember the conviction was overturned on appeal.

Afterwards, I couldn't bear to face her – Lily, Mrs Chin – and she couldn't bear to stay in the US. She already had her ticket back to China when the first verdict came out, but it only delayed things. She finally went back forty years after she left. Went home, some might say, to Canton, though by then it was called Guangzhou. She used to say she couldn't remain in a land of injustice, but I always thought it was the vicious ironies that drove her out. She'd left China, after all, to escape her memories of the Japanese invasion, only to have her son killed because he was mistaken for a Japanese, and then to make common cause with Japanese-Americans in her search for justice.

'Toyota, Datsun, Honda... Pearl Harbor,' went a popular Detroit bumper sticker back in the day. Ten years after Vincent's death, Lee Iacocca, Chrysler's president and pitchman, was still complaining that the Japanese were 'beating our brains in'. Recently, I read Buick was a bestseller in China.

I wonder how Mrs Chin might have felt seeing American cars on the roads there. She lived in China another twenty years, but came back to the US for cancer treatment at the end of her life. The Asian-American Rosa Parks, the obits called her. She's buried between Vincent and his father.

They asked me to her funeral too, as they've asked me faithfully to anniversaries, and conferences and rallies down the years, as they've asked me to this latest memorial. I appreciate the sentiment. They forgive me – for lying or not lying well enough, either way. If only I could forgive myself. But it's too late for the truth now. You can't say all this stuff at an unveiling, in a documentary or an interview. You can't say all this when someone calls you a motherfucker.

I RSVP'd my regrets this morning. I can't, and never could, save the day.

Lily used to say, *Vincent still be live if I hadn't adopted him.* I should have talked to her; we were the two who felt most guilty, the ones who most wanted someone else to pay. This afternoon at least I went to her grave, all their graves, cleaned the stones, left oranges and lit joss. The sod over Vincent and his father is a shade greener than that over his mother's more recent plot, like jade that darkens from wearing.

There's a Canton near Detroit as it happens (pronounced '*Cant*en' which is why I didn't think about it for years). You pass signs for it on the way to the cemetery. A little research tells me there used to be a local Pekin and a Nankin, too – all named in the 1830s, when the nation was fascinated by all things Chinese, before any Chinese had arrived. There are Cantons all across the country dating from the same period in Ohio, Mississippi, Georgia, Kansas, Texas. The Canton in South Dakota was said to be on the exact other side of the world from its namesake.

Sometimes I wonder if anything might have been different if I'd not gone along that night. Different for me, of course – how I've wished I was never there – but also for him. I'd never been to the Fancy Pants with him before, but I'd heard about it. It was one reason I jumped at the chance. Why hadn't he asked me along before? He'd taken Jerry and Bill. He might have been worried I'd blab, tell mutual friends, that it'd get back to Vicki, I guess, but it's not like he didn't brag about it. No, I think, it was something else. I wasn't as cool as him, you might say, and I wasn't, but really any Chinese is less cool alongside another. Maybe we lose our exoticism. More likely, it's that alone, we can define ourselves, with another we invite all the stereotypes. Alone, or especially with Jerry or Bill, he was Vince. With me alongside, he was Vincent, Asian. So, I have to ask, would Evans have called us names, if there'd only been one of us. 'It's because of you…' he said, and he meant us, you *plural*. One isn't a threat, two or more… well, we were *them*. And would Vincent have gotten so angry if I hadn't been there? Perhaps, probably. But just maybe he felt he had to represent, answer back. He knew I wouldn't – later, when the bouncers intervened, I even tried to apologize to Evans, play peacemaker – so Vincent may have figured it fell to him to uphold our honour, even protect *me*. Then again, maybe he just didn't want to be like me. Maybe he yelled back, threw the first punch, to prove we weren't the same. 'I'm not a motherfucker,' he said. He didn't say, '*We're* not.'

There's a name for it, OK, this idea we all look alike. It's been studied, documented. *Cross-race bias*, they call it. It's true of how whites see blacks; even how other races see whites. But with Asians the sameness is magnified. There are so many of us! Squeezed together in our over-crowded cities. And we all have the same names! And dress alike, wear glasses (I kept mine on to look at the girls; Vincent wore contacts). Even the things we make are copies – cheap knock-offs, poor imitations. We may all look alike, but when we try to copy you… well, the differences are obvious (and if they're not, it just means we're getting trickier, not to be trusted). Maybe to Evans and Pitts, Vincent was just a pale imitation. Maybe the reason they killed him is not because he was like me, but because he was trying to be like them.

If I had a gun I'd shoot you now, I told Evans while we waited for the ambulance, but I didn't of course.

And what about all the other what ifs? Ten thousand of them, as Evans said. What if none of us had gone that night? Or not gotten so drunk? Not cared what a couple of assholes said? What if I hadn't run? And what if the judge locked those guys up at the first trial? What if justice was seen to be done? Vincent is still dead, Lily still goes back to China, Vicki is still alone, I'm still yellow. It's a tragedy, but a small one, forgotten in time. But the verdict, the paltry fines, that's what made travesty of tragedy. Shit, it's a toss-up which was more racist: the crime or the verdict. But it's the injustice that lives on, the unfairness that ensures Vincent's death will be remembered. And alongside it, always and for ever, my cowardice, like a bass line, a footnote, minor but essential. His friend who ran away. Martyrs and saints, you see, they have to be brave. Otherwise they're just victims. Vincent could have run away. That's what my life proves. He chose not to. Never mind that he *should* have run. He had a mother to care for, a wife to live for. Never mind that he was a hothead, who didn't give any more thought to his loved ones than he had in the club. No. He stood up, before he was knocked down. And I ran.

Yin to his yang (if you want to fit it in a fortune cookie).

He's a symbol now. His prom picture on T-shirts, posters, his name a rallying cry. And yet he can't symbolise *me*. For him to mean what he means, he and I have to be different.

As the old joke goes:

Two Chinamen going down the street.
One of them walks into a club.
The other one ducks.

(Not funny?) Maybe it's the way I tell 'em.

We'd been sitting outside the McDonald's on Woodward, perched on a raised planter made out of old railroad ties, our panting turning to laughter. We thought we'd lost them. 'Your face when he pulled out that bat!' 'I thought I was gonna shit myself, OK?' It was becoming a story. I could see us telling it at the wedding. I could see us joking about it for years to come. And it was just the two of us, something we'd always share. Evans and Pitts had ignored Jerry and Bill, after all. They only chased us. We sat shoulder to shoulder, sharing a smoke. In a minute I was going to suggest a Big Mac and fries (Vincent would likely counter with a Coney Dog from Red Hots up the block, another old haunt).

Saturday night, ten something, sidewalks still warm from the sun. Six lanes of traffic came and went in the intersection before us, exhaust rising redly in the tail lights.

'First car in Detroit drove down this street,' he said.

'First mile of concrete paving in the country,' I recited from some high school field trip. 'First assembly line rolled 'em out, right over there.'

'My dad used to bring me down here to watch the cruising when I was a kid, teach me the names of all the marques. He could still remember the streetcars running. Now I can remember when it was all elms along here.'

The last time I'd seen him, I realised, was at his father's funeral.

'I don't even want a Jap car,' he said. 'It'd be like a Jew buying a Beamer!'

'Me either.'

'What would you drive if you could have any car?'

I actually wanted an Audi, but what I said was, 'Trans-Am.'

'Sally Fields in the passenger seat?' he teased. 'You always loved them pony cars.'

'What about you?'

Cars were stopping in the intersection again.

'Porsche, man! Black 911 Turbo Carrera. What else?'

We were still laughing when they spotted us. 'Sitting there and laughing,' Evans said in court. 'It must have been real funny to them.' A joke at his expense, I guess he figured.

I haven't bought an American car in thirty years. I've never been to a baseball game. I have been back to a strip club once. The night after the final acquittal. This was in Cincinnati. Evans' lawyers had successfully petitioned for a change of venue. It would be impossible to get a fair trial in Detroit after all the publicity about the case – interviews Lily had given, they argued, were 'prejudicial' – even though publicity was the only reason the case had gotten reopened in the first place. At jury selection, I'd heard, fewer than 10 per cent of possible Cincinnati jurors said they'd ever met an Asian-American.

The place was called Sin City. Nicer than the Fancy Pants, it smelled of Windex and warm vinyl, a chemical new car whiff, but I figured I could still get in trouble there. I was the one spoiling for a fight now, fantasising about Evans and Pitts walking in to celebrate, tightening my grip on the neck of my beer, feeling the pulse in my fist. I watched the girls, one reminded me a little of Lacey, and I watched the men watching them. But no one seemed to notice me. The mood was mild, sappy even. Worn, lonely men in rumpled sport coats, eyes wide and watery from drink, grinning like kids on

Christmas. I wondered, could that have been Vincent if he'd lived? Lacey had said he was always smiling. By contrast, I was the one sourpuss in there, and the girls seemed to know to steer clear. If anyone was going to start something in there, it was going to be me, but I realised after a while I'd simply be too embarrassed to make a scene. The rowdiest it got was some joker waving his lighter in the air, shouting *Freebird!* until a bouncer shushed him primly, a finger to his lips. The crowd was mostly white, the bouncers all black, the girls a mix, even one Asian girl dancing to 'Turning Japanese' (a euphemism for masturbation, so I'd heard, though it might have been BS). She came out like a geisha, mincing in a shiny kimono; by the end all she was wearing was white make-up and bright red lipstick. I found myself blushing for her, as I thought, unable to watch except out of the corner of my eye, but then I realised I was ashamed for myself, praying she wouldn't see *me*, come over. Expose me.

She couldn't have made me out in the gloom, I told myself. We men must have just been a constellation of cigarette tips from the stage.

Thirty minutes later she did another set, this one in a sleek black wig to 'China Girl'. And this time I did study her, her face, trying to decide.

Towards the end of her set, when she was naked, she met my eyes and I realised she'd known I was there all along, had seen me during her first set, or from backstage. Afterwards, she came up to me at the bar, wrapped in a short robe, nipples showing through like rivets. I shivered, reminded of how chilled the place was. 'Don't

I know you, hun?' I swallowed my drink, shook my head, made to leave, but she put her hand on my arm. 'What's your name?'

'Vincent.' It just came out in my panic. I might have flinched, but if she noticed it was only because she was used to people lying.

'Well, Vinny, I'm Cindy. Wanna buy me a drink?'

'Can I ask, are you Chinese or Japanese?'

'Whatever you want me to be, baby.'

'No really. Tell me.'

'You wanna guess?' she asked, still teasing.

'No!'

'OK, baby, OK.' She was calculating, I thought, trying to decide what I wanted to hear, even though I didn't even know myself. And something else – as reluctant to reveal herself as she'd be to tell me her real name.

And suddenly, I didn't want her to have to lie.

'It's fine,' I told her, finishing my drink. 'It doesn't matter.'

But she smiled, put a hand on my arm. 'All American, baby. We're all American here.'

It felt like something to cover ourselves in, that word, its warm anonymity. And I nodded, sank back on my stool, bought her that drink.

NOT LIKE ME

Look Not with the Eyes

Damian Barr

There's something to see.

People are stopping even in the not-quite-rain. They lower their Asda bags carefully to the pavement, tins pushing against the sides so you can read the labels through the plastic. There are enough backs to the main parade to make me wonder what's going on. It's not a fight, there's no shouting, no sides. It could be a fight that's finished but there's old people so it's probably not and nobody's leaving. They're all watching as one.

A Saturday in almost October and the villages have caught the bus to town to do their shopping and see who's who and what's what. Motherwell is mobbed. My mum is somewhere in the Asda stretching her Wednesday money to the three of us and her useless boyfriend. As usual I'm headed to the John Menzies in search of a Stephen King the library's not got yet – *Misery* took me four Saturdays cross-legged on the sticky vinyl floor avoiding looks from the manager. There's no new King today and the stories in the papers are not as big as the stories on our street so I wander out. It's spitting on my specs so I take them off for a wipe. When I put them back on I notice the not-quite-crowd by the grey patch of rubble where I dream a McDonald's will one day open.

'Are they clowns or what?' one rain-bonneted head asks another as I edge over.

'Ah don't know,' her pal shrugs, leaning heavily on her tartan shopping trolley. 'When's the 91 due?'

As they turn towards the bus stop I eye their place, judging the people either side – do they know me? Do they know about me? There's laughing from the front like somebody's watching the telly. That kind of laugh's all right. I step forward. No need to stand on tiptoe – I'm fourteen and already over six foot but not as tall as my dad. Not yet. I only see him every two weeks now so he notices me stretching. Gro-bag, he calls me. That's a nice name. My mum's got to jump up now to ruffle my hair. She says it needs a shear or folk will think I'm a hippy or something. Or something. I never want to stand out but right now my height – the height my dad gave me – is useful. Here's what I see.

There are four people, two men and two women, all old enough to be working. The younger of the two men has shoulder-length curls so at first I think he's one of the girls, and the younger girl's got a crew cut so at first I think she's one of the boys. They're all wearing blue dungarees and bright white T-shirts. I've never seen them before. Any of them. Not from the window of the 91. Not in the Asda. Not even in the *Motherwell Times*. They are strangers.

Curly steps forward then lies down on the rubble and closes his eyes and goes straight to sleep the way people do in films. But this is not the pictures. He folds his hands under his head and the rubble must be digging in but you can't tell from his face. I hear his breathing. Crew-cut tiptoes over from behind and looks at us all one by one and when she gets to me I nearly duck because what if she sees. A man sniggers awkwardly and winks back and more men join in but she's not bothered. When she's sure we're all looking she pulls a tiny green bottle from her dungaree pocket and holds it up, unstopping it with a swoop. She kneels down and drips it into Curly's eyes. Curly sleeps on. I stand bewitched.

'I've got night shift and I'm no missin the bus for this,' says the guy in front of me, turning to go. His wife hooks him back with a sharp elbow. 'Shhsht,' she says. 'They're doin somethin.' Her husband huffs and lights a Benson & Hedges. He blows smoke at Curly.

Crew-cut murmurs something in Curly's ear but he doesn't stir. I want to brush the curls from over his ear and whisper *sorry about the smoke*. As I lean forward the wife gives in and her husband gives me a look as they mutter off to the stop where the 91 is pulling up. The audience is halving but Crew-cut doesn't stop. She gets louder so we can all hear. 'What thou seest, when thou dost wake, Do it for thy true-love take.'

Words from English! Said out loud! Here, in Motherwell town centre! I want to tell them all *I know, I know what she's saying, this is Shakespeare and she's a fairy!* I imagine myself saying *fairy* out loud and end the thought, make myself as small as I can.

Crew-cut tilts her chin at us. She tiptoes backwards without looking away and waits. I wonder how much longer I've got before my mum comes out the Asda and asks me to help with the bags. I close my eyes and will her to forget something, to have to turn her trolley back, it never goes the way she wants it to anyway.

The older man, whose chest hair is escaping from the top of his T-shirt, pulls something from a bag at his feet. It's a mask of a donkey. He puts it on and trots about going *Ee!Aw! Ee!Aw!* Some wee ones at the front clap and join in and their mothers don't know if they should stop them or not because this is not school but it's not your normal Saturday afternoon in Motherwell either. Donkey dances on. I wonder how fast he can run. The 91 pulls away in a plume of diesel smoke.

Finally, Curly wakes slowly like he's been sleeping for a thousand years, like me on a Sunday after I've been up all night with a book. He rubs his eyes with his knuckles. When Donkey dances by his whole face changes. He blinks and there's a light in his eyes. He clasps both hands over his heart and jumps up with just his legs and shouts 'Love!' More nervous laughter. I smile then remember to tut.

Who are these people? Where have they come from? Curly follows Donkey round telling him how much he loves him. They're not scared, they're not even embarrassed. I blush for them. I try to work their accent out. It's not from a hundred miles of here. It's not even English. It's like American. They've come all the way here from all the way somewhere else for this. Curly reaches for Donkey's hand and I have to stop myself slapping it away. But nobody's doing anything, not yet. I want everybody to stop shuffling and pay attention and actually look like they're paying attention and one or two do. The rain finally gives in and the sun makes a cameo so the wet grey rubble almost sparkles. Coats are undone.

Now all four of them are talking over and through one another and it's hard to keep up, like following a row from upstairs. Who did what and who loves who and what will happen next? I can't remember the ending but I can't stop watching. My mum has to be done now. She'll be getting rung up, watching the number on the till getting bigger and feeling her purse get lighter. I should help her with the bags, I should.

Enough people have left now that I'm right at the front. There's an invisible line between them and us. Between me and everybody else. I can feel it. I know I've got to go. But I want to stay till the end, till after the end when everybody's left and it's just me and them and Donkey lifts his mask off and comes over and does a bow and I copy him and they all applaud me and when they offer me a drop from that little green bottle I'll take it. I'll take it and I'll go with them. I'll go.

Bodies

Sam Guglani

Others followed but the first was your father, in a front room, in amber light, mourners gathered in chorus, the shock of his skin like the coffin kept different air.

You recover him today, decades on, in a white shirt, in sweat and song, dust and stories – baby Krishna, night-blue, eating the soil in his garden, Yashoda opening his mouth, the universe glimmering in it. Or Hanuman, look, brave ape, peeling his chest and fur like it's ripe fruit – soft tissues, ribs, the found kernel of a heart, bloody and beating and traced with faces, visions.

Stories of gods and us, shaped from muscle and cloud and mud, threaded substance of flesh, human and animal and other.

But your body is only a shirt, he'd say, look at it fall away.

And is this what brings you here? To this work? Asking what a body is? How it stops mid breath? How his stopped mid breath? Are you here to study this trick of animation, gaze held like a stethoscope to the living, the dead, the steadily dying?

It startles you at times, that matter orchestrates to life, aches on you like the light of blossom – glimpsed for a moment in a body's thinned skin that creases to a wink, or its casual throw of some thirty bones into a hand's perfect gesture.

Is it grief, the ache, or is it wonder?

It swells the view, the way dusk swells a landscape.

Enlarges it from a person, a hospital bed, to a pattern of all bodies, and here, to your own – its quiet tap of pulse and breath now loud, its bones both heavy and tenuous, and its limbs oddly estranged, as if hung from someone other, someone elsewhere. Look, even your movements seem foreign, a puppet's feint – your arms unfolding to another, the mechanical press of a kiss.

You are startled in truth by luck, the fall of it, how fickle drifts of matter dictate a life's wayward course, gift it attrition or suffering with such indifference – startled at your own unearned reprieve, from a puncture of needles, say, or bullets, a sheer weight of rubble or ocean or loss.

Old men, you're told, should be explorers. Then you, afforded this view, might be more capable of presence, of reverence or apology or attention – to this flickering of life, its continuum of breakages and brevity, its fragile luminescence, to others, more capable at least of love.

Things Unspoken

Sara Nović

Everything that moves makes a sound, my mother told me once.

It was her response to a firestorm of test cases, me running around our house pointing and saying, How about that? How about that?

Everything, she said.

Of course there are the obvious examples: feet stomping, drawers shutting, vibrations I can feel. But with other things – the ceiling fan, the flicking of switches and igniting of bulbs – I'm not so sure. Now, sitting bored on the floor behind the reception desk at her studio, I wonder if it's even true. I scan the room for traces of noise, but the students haven't shown up yet and everything is still.

Through the front window the neon sign flickers: YMEDACA ECNAD YDAL RIAF YM

Maybe light really does make a sound. Or maybe she just said it to shut me up.

Noisy or not, the girly name isn't doing me any favours. It's bad enough I have to spend my afterschools at a dance studio, but I can't even pretend they're doing something cool back there – hip-hop, or that Spanish dancing where the partners look like they're going to punch each other – not with a name like that. The guys at school make fun of me: Chris-sy the sissy, Chris-sy the sissy.

Even my father used to say, Melinda, a dance studio is no place for a boy to be spending his time.

But he took off and my mom says his opinion doesn't count any more. No, she says, you are only twelve; I don't want you home alone that much.

From the outside this place is a dumpy storefront, occupying the better part of the strip mall across the road from our house. Inside it is clean and bright and people bring their kids even from East Somerton, two towns over, because my mom was a famous dancer in New York City until she got hurt and wasn't any more.

At twenty to five the skeletors enter in a cloud of hairspray and gossip. My mother's best dancers. They are high school seniors, skinny skinny skinny – their waists up too high, their necks too long, arms and legs drawn out like silly putty. Still, there is something about them that makes me want to brush up against them when we pass in the hallway. But they never let me touch them.

I glance up at the old lady who mans the front desk. I didn't even notice her come in but now she's staring at me, blowing hot air in the shape of my name as if she hasn't known me since I was two, as if she has no idea I can't hear. I watch her blotchy cheeks expand and contract as she puffs out breath that smells like rotten fruit. She has chin hair.

Chris, move, I need to file these and you're in the way.

I stand up. She dumps a stack of papers into the fat bottom drawer of the desk.

I dodge a cluster of manic preschoolers in tutus and turn the corner into the kitchen, where I jump up and sit on the counter. The skeletors are there, pretending to eat and monitoring how much they are each not eating. In school we learned about eating disorders, but doctors should take a look in here to witness this medical marvel: anorexia as a social event. I swing my legs so the heels of my sneakers bang against the cabinet doors. I know this makes a noise and that it's an annoying one.

Stop, Chris, you're giving us a headache, one says, like they have a single collective head I can inflict pain upon.

How do you say, Me and my boyfriend are gonna be together for everrrrr, in sign language? another one asks.

Like this, I say with my mouth. But with my hands I say, Your boyfriend wishes you had tits.

They copy my motion and giggle.

When I finish my homework I slip through the side door of the big classroom and clean the bathrooms, reducing the time lag between when classes are finished and when we can go home. The girls are in ballet now, and I watch as they glissade diagonally across the room, two-by-two, Noah's ark meets *Attack of the Clones*: sissonne – pas de chat – plié – pirouette. Over the years I've learned all the ballet terms there are to know. They are, after all, my mother's words.

At the end of the night my mother is sweaty, blonde hair plastered to her head like the skin of an onion. The fabric of her shirt is almost see-through in the part stretched across her pregnant belly.

Chris, carry that for me? She points to a box full of pink baby clothes.

What is it?

Hand-me-downs, she says.

We don't know if the baby is a boy or a girl, and the box of frilly outfits makes me nervous. I stare. She points again, though we both know I've understood.

My mother doesn't know sign language. She read in her parenting magazines that kids who signed would never learn to speak. Then, after I'd learned both and proved her wrong, she declared signing unnecessary.

You talk. You read lips.

I've spent my whole life reading her, extracting meaning from the twitch of her cheek, the crease between her eyebrows. But we only know one another through our second languages, our thoughts ordered by separate dictionaries.

When we get home Greg is on the couch, relaxing, he calls it, except that he is still wearing his tie all the way up, tight around his neck. Greg is a schmuck. I know because I had a tie – the real kind, not a clip on – when my parents went to family court. Ties are not for relaxing.

Hiya, Sport, he says, which is another thing about him.

Hi, Schmuck, my hands say. My mouth just says, Hi, Greg.

Every night he turns off the captions on the TV and every night when I ask him to turn them back on he looks surprised, as if he forgot I lived here too, or expected me to come home from the studio cured and whistling a show tune.

Did you take care of your mother for me?

Not for you, my hands say. I scrubbed the toilets, I say out loud. Good man, Greg says.

My mother sits down next to him on the couch, tries to pry her boot from her swollen ankle. Greg watches from the corner of his eye but does nothing, continues fondling the remote. I grab the boot and pull. It comes loose and the heel jabs me in the stomach.

Thank you, Chris, my mother says.

Good man, Greg says, and changes the channel.

Greg passes by my room as I am getting into bed. He leans in the doorway, watching. His shoulders rise up, then drop in a sigh.

Goodnight, Sport.

Schmuck. He grabs my doorknob and starts to pull.

No, no, I say, I need it open; I need to see.

Oh, right, Greg says. I stand in the shadows by my bed, waiting for him to go away so I can put things back the way they're supposed to be.

I wake in the middle of the night, knowing before I know. Lights on in other rooms, their glow meeting in the hallway outside my open door. Still I've learned not to get out of bed in the hours that belong to grown-ups, hours when fathers come home drunk and bruises ripen. I seal my eyelids down in fake sleep. Then I feel my mother's clammy hand on my shoulder telling me it's OK to be awake.

It's time to go, she says.

I stumble around on unsteady morning feet looking for my sneakers. The sky is navy blue and the roads are empty. My mother breathes like she's been underwater for too long and I think please

please please be a girl. A daughter with rubber-band muscles and an ear for music. A girl who my mother can teach to dance, and can make her smile her real smile again, the one with teeth she only shows by accident when she's laughing.

I'm in a waiting room where they keep the expecting grandparents. They're wheeling my mom away and she is yelling at the receptionist, He's deaf, he's deaf, just so you know. The floor is waxed and the reflection of the lights looks like flying saucers.

I shuffle through stacks of magazines, the kinds that only exist in doctors' offices. What's Wrong With This Picture? What's Wrong With This Picture? After a while, all the pictures start to look ridiculous. I fall asleep sideways in one of those extra-wide chairs made for fat people. Greg wakes me up.

Come see her.

I wonder if Her means my mother, or if the baby is out and it's a girl. At first I'm afraid to walk into the room but when I do my mother is sitting up in bed holding a big ball of blanket and it is pink!

Thank you! I actually say aloud and Greg and my mother look at me funny so I say, How is everything, how do you feel, what are you going to name her?

We'll call her Skylar, for her big blue eyes.

Skylar is a word I've never said before. I test it out, rolling the syllables around on my tongue. My science book says babies' eyes can change colour as they get older, but the name feels sweet in my mouth so I say nothing.

I figure out Skylar is deaf long before everyone else. She and my mom come home from the hospital, and I spend lots of time in Skylar's pink nursery, just looking at her. Once her eyes start to open wider she looks back at me. I hold her in the crook of my arm, sign a word or two with my other hand, and her eyes narrow and focus like the lens of a camera. I put her back in her cradle and clap behind her head, watch her not react. I think I should tell my mother, but when I get downstairs I find her in the kitchen among gifts – flowered onesies and pastel stuffed animals. She is smiling. I go back to Skylar's room.

Just me and you, Sky, I say, my hands useful in this house for the first time. Don't worry. I've got you.

They find out at Skylar's six-month check-up. I sit in the waiting room, and when my mother comes out and tells me I clamp my back teeth together and think don't move a muscle, now is not the time to be talkative.

Impossible impossible, she says in the car.

When Greg comes home my mother hugs him and cries until her snot drips down the back of his shirt. I sit with Skylar and show her nursery rhymes. I tell her the one where the dish and the spoon take off together and she giggles like we are sharing a secret.

Don't worry, Greg says. We can fix this.

Soon Skylar's tiny hands begin to form baby-talk signs of their own. I love watching my words on her fingertips. Eat, she says. Eat, more, drink, more. Mom. Mom, mom. Dad. Chris, she says, her hand crunched into a 'C' and pressed against her chest. Chris. It's her clearest sign of all.

I have to talk to you, my mother says one night, and I think shit they've mailed home my report card. I follow her into her bedroom and she makes me sit down. I am waiting for her to say no video games for a week, but instead she says:

You need to know that girls can be unkind. You need to know the way I hurt myself in the ballet was not an accident.

Oh no, I say, because my mother has deployed this kind of story before, a tactical pity bomb preceding something she knows I'll hate, but she keeps going.

She tells me how she'd gotten the attention of the grey-haired Russians in the audition hall that winter, that she'd been selected to dance the principal duet with an already famous man-dancer, that she was going to be famous, too. I know this part of the story.

But the other girls were jealous. They starved themselves; they ate toilet paper and vomited and got even thinner. They cut skinnier girls' hair at night, just enough so the victims couldn't form the mandatory bun without shorter bits slipping out from under the elastic and pins. It was an environment in which my mother should have known to look inside her pointe shoes for acts of sabotage. Instead, when she stepped into the pink satin during her quick-change in dress rehearsal, the razor blades standing at attention inside met her flesh and left her big toes flayed open like a pair of raw sausages. They healed eventually, but by then she'd been replaced.

I'm telling you this so you can understand, she says. We're going to get Skylar a cochlear implant.

This whole time I have been silent but now I feel myself yelling, You can't, you can't, they'll drill a hole in her skull!

We have an appointment at the clinic next week, she says. Everything will be OK.

Skylar is not like you, I want to say. Skylar is perfect. But the words shrivel in my mouth and I think I might throw up so I run down the hall into the bathroom and stand with my face over the toilet. Nothing happens, and my mother doesn't come after me.

I want to get out of the house and I look around and why the hell do I always lose my goddamn sneakers? When I find them I pull them on and slink from room to room, trying to pin down the location of my mother and Greg. I've memorised every place I've gotten caught before and I avoid all the loose floorboards. I peek back in my mother's room, where she is sitting on her bed matching socks, the phone squeezed between her shoulder and chin.

I know, Mom, she says. So I keep watching, trying to guess what my grandma might be saying to her, hoping that she'll tell my mother that Skylar is fine. My mother is holding in her crying now, her nose red and flaring at the tip.

And to think, she says. All this time I thought it was Him.

She rubs her forehead with the heel of her hand. As surprised as my mother is that she carries silence in her own veins, I am just as shaken by the reminder that I have my father's angry blood inside of me.

I feel jittery again and mean to run right down the stairs and out the front door but instead find myself walking toward Skylar's room. She's asleep in her crib and I pick her up and throw her extra blanket over my shoulder.

Outside the air is cool and I feel better. We can go anywhere we want, Sky, I tell her, but it's dark and she's asleep, and even I know I'm lying. I wait for a gap in the headlights and run across the highway, Skylar's little head bobbing against my shoulder.

At the strip mall I decide I am never going in that stupid dance school ever again, which I prove by walking past a few times, up and down the sidewalk and around the parking lot. Then I get a little closer for a quick look. I pull on the door handle, jiggling it hard; I kick the bottom metal part and hurt my toe. I turn around to go home. But then I feel the place behind me, the big ugly MY FAIR LADY flashing out a rhythm that looks like a laugh, and I can't let it get away with that. I hoist Skylar up higher, feel her breath quicken against my neck. Then I take a rock from the parking lot, a chunk of asphalt rough in my palm, and throw it hard, a SMASH through the front window. I reach through the broken glass and release the lock on the other side, let us in.

I know there is a burglar alarm and we don't have a lot of time, so I go straight into the studio and swing my free hand through the giant stack of CDs in the corner, smash them too, jumbo-sized Jenga. I pick one off the top of the pile and slide it into the stereo. It's a fancy system, a lot of levers and dials, and I just turn them all up to where they stop twisting and lay down in front of the speaker. The sound ripples on my windbreaker and up my spine; Skylar, pressed against me, doesn't wake up. Music banging hard inside my ribcage, music like a heart attack. Red siren light streaks along the spidered glass and the vibration swells through my chest and up into hers. The room swirls and flashes and smells like feet, and I breathe the bass line, and wait for someone to find me.

Excuse Me, but Your Otherness Is Showing

Joanne Limburg

There was always something other about me, and people noticed it. They couldn't have said what it was they were noticing, but they sensed it in the room. I noticed them noticing. Sometimes, as I was walking down a street, or through a corridor, I would register that this person or that was visibly disconcerted by looking into my face; sometimes they looked bewildered; sometimes they seemed uncomfortable and shrank back. It was the nameless something at work. Some people sensed it as vulnerability, explaining things to me very slowly and carefully, or asking me if I was all right; sometimes people interpreted what they sensed as a physical fragility and insisted on carrying things for me when I hadn't asked. Some people caught it as predators catch the scent of prey. Some felt repulsed or a little threatened and shunned it. Most people, at least some of the time, laughed at it. A few were drawn towards it, and when they laughed, laughed with it.

I remember how it bewildered the medical student I met at a

mutual friend's party in the early 1990s. We had been talking for about fifteen minutes or so, when she asked, apropos of nothing, 'So do you do something artistic? Are you an artist, or a writer?' I said I wrote poetry. 'Ah, I see,' she said. 'I thought it must be something like that.' She said this with satisfaction and some relief, as she might when a consultant had asked her a question about a patient during a ward round, and she had got the answer right.

And she wasn't wrong: I did define myself as a writer. I hadn't published any writing at that point, let alone earned anything from it (unless you count the £10 book token I'd won in a Puffin Club poetry competition some years earlier), but I felt at my most comfortable when I was communicating via a screen or a page. When I wrote, I could devote my whole energy to thinking about exactly what I wanted my words to mean, without having to worry about how I'd approach all the hurdles that littered my spoken interactions. I didn't have to worry about whether, or how, it would be appropriate to initiate a conversation; I didn't have to address two listeners at once; I didn't have to follow the conversation like a musician might have to follow an unseen orchestral score, anxiously waiting for the right moment to come in; I didn't have to judge when it was the right moment to leave the conversation; I didn't have to concern myself with the possibility that, in my face, or voice, or posture, or clothes, or some other aspect of my appearance, my non-specific otherness might be showing. The page never did a double take, never laughed at me, never flinched or frowned or criticised; it never exchanged smirks with an adjacent page, or whispered to it behind its hand; it never pinned me to a wall at a party and demanded to know why

I refused to have sex with it. So if the otherness was being a writer, there was some compensation.

At the time of the party, in the early nineties, another form of words to describe the otherness – a more medical form of words, suitable for use on a ward round – was beginning to gain currency in the English-speaking world. It would take another twenty years before I understood how the words applied to me. I hadn't heard of Asperger's Syndrome. I had heard of autism, but, like most people, assumed that it was rare, and invariably meant absent or very limited speech, an apparent lack of emotional response to other people and a complete inability to care for oneself. Other people, meanwhile, didn't seem to talk about autistic people as though they *were* people. To be autistic, I learned, was, by definition, to be empty in some way; autistic people lacked language, symbolic thought, empathy, social knowhow – the ingredients that human beings like to think define them as human. It was fine to write about them as if they'd never read it. It was perfectly reasonable to talk about them as if they'd never hear.

Being talked about as if one were not in the room – being objectified – is an experience most of us have had from time to time. Most of us have probably done it to someone else. We do it, routinely, to children ('Doesn't he look like you!'; 'Hasn't she grown!'; 'They're both doing ever so well!'). Medical staff have traditionally done it to patients, not infrequently on ward rounds. Along with the vast majority of other women and some men, I've experienced it as part of street harassment ('Did you see her tits?'). It is at best awkward, and at worst utterly dehumanising. Like children, disabled adults experience it routinely; unlike children, they cannot look forward to a natural endpoint.

It was partly the wish to avoid this – the humiliation of being talked about as if I were not in the room – that drove me to try to identify that thing about me that made people react so badly, to identifying it with a view to obliterating it. When I was playing an improvisation game in a drama lesson, and another girl made a pointed comment about a character's wearing 'white knee socks', at which everyone but me laughed, I took a quick look round at all the legs in the circle and made a mental note to change what I wore on mine. When I was hurrying to an appointment at university, heard laughter in front of me and then a voice behind me saying, 'What's funny? Is it her running?' I made a further note, to run as little possible in public. When I attempted to join a conversation at my first workplace by telling a story that started with the phrase 'You know, once…' and one of the people I was trying to talk to turned to the others and said, 'You know, once – fuck, I forgot what I was going to say, but I'm sure it was a *hilarious fucking anecdote*,' I became positively phobic about using that particular opener ever again. A few months later, I was discreetly – I thought – reading a book and eating a sandwich on the Tube on the way home; this time the shriek of laughter came from a woman a few seats along. She explained me to her friend: 'FIRST she opens her mouth, then she picks a bit out of her teeth, then she looks at it, then she flicks it away!' It was news to me as well as to her friend: I had forgotten to remind myself that I was visible to other people even when I wasn't looking at them. It seemed to me that every one of these little humiliations had come about because I had failed to keep an eye on my otherness; it had peeped out in the way that I dressed, or ran, or spoke, or ate a sandwich, and in doing so it had made me fair game. I had allowed it to give the signal that I wasn't quite human enough to deserve fully human consideration.

These are all moments from my teens and twenties, and I now see them as autistic moments. They all took place decades before I was diagnosed; it isn't a diagnosis in and of itself that renders people like me other. It's the perception of difference, of a failure to conform in some way to all those tiny, unspoken rules around appearance, demeanour and behaviour that become visible only in the breach. You only need to have the wrong facial expression, the wrong conversational rhythm, the wrong way of sitting, the wrong gait when you run. You only need to be a bit absent-minded about the way you eat a sandwich. You only need to react, as I often do, half a beat too late.

Recently I began teaching on a course which has Stephen King's book, *On Writing*, as a set text. It was my first Stephen King. (I don't tend to read or watch horror – as you may have gathered, I experience quite enough unpredictable threat in my life without going out of my way to find it.) Most of the book is taken up with thoughts about the writing process, but it begins on a more personal note, with a section called 'CV', in which King touches on the experiences that formed him as a writer. Some of these appear as slight fragments of memory; others are considered at greater length. One of the longer sub-sections explores the genesis of his first published novel, *Carrie*. He explains that its title character, the teenage outcast who enacts a horrific, telekinetic revenge on her tormentors, grew out of his uneasy memories of two girls he knew during his own high school years. They were two girls who looked wrong, sounded wrong, *smelled* wrong. They dressed in the wrong clothes. Both came from homes which were thought to be strange but what made them – in King's words – 'two loneliest and most reviled' of the girls in his class was something less tangible than background. Returning to the subject in his introduction to an edition of *Carrie*, he suggests that this was a something 'that broadcast *STRANGE! NOT LIKE US! KEEP AWAY!*'

King speculates that this broadcast occupied a 'wavelength only other kids can pick up', but I'm not so sure that people ever grow out of its reception. They might learn to respond to it less unkindly, but they still sense it. It seemed to me, reading this, that the something King describes is not only his reviled classmates' something, and his character Carrie's something, but *my* something too. Unless I take deliberate steps to dampen the signal, I broadcast discomfort. Delving into the scholarly literature around *Carrie*, King and the horror genre, I came across a word that had been at the back of my mind for some time – not a diagnostic word like 'autistic' or 'Asperger's' – but a word for what Freud describes as an 'aesthetic experience'. It's a great word: 'uncanny'.

The dictionary definition of 'uncanny' is 'strange and difficult to explain'. If you look back to the beginning of this essay, you'll see that, as someone who appears a bit off for no clearly discernible reason, I fit the definition pretty well. In his paper on the uncanny, Freud quotes another psychiatrist, Ernst Jentsch, who writes that 'one of the most successful devices for easily creating uncanny effects is to leave the reader in uncertainty whether a particular figure in the story is a human being or automaton'. Bear that quote in mind, and think back again, to the part where I talked about autistic people not being seen as fully human. One of the hard lessons of my life has been the realisation that to register automatically as a fellow human to other human beings, it is not enough to have a human body, a mind, a capacity of experience and suffering, to bleed, laugh and all the rest, if somehow the way one holds oneself, walks, dresses, speaks, and arranges the various features and muscles of one's face fail to combine in such a way as to signal, 'I'm one of you'. Humanity, in our casual encounters, is not something we intuit in the depths of our being, but something we read off the surface.

My response to this has been to spend a huge amount of time and energy adjusting and tuning my surface so that it reads more easily, so that I can, as Carrie puts it, 'get along with the world' and in doing so become 'a whole person'. I don't always succeed, of course, because no amount of conscious adjustment can fully compensate for a set of defaults that one doesn't have. And you might be reading this, and thinking, 'But you're already a person!' And you'd be right. And you'd be right that all the other autistic people are already whole too. But we're not always treated as such, and until we are, you'll understand that I'll carry on being watchful, and reading, and thinking, and trying in every way I can to figure out why.

We Are the Champions

Salena Godden

As I begin this essay I'm acutely aware you may have seen the
title of this book and said to yourself, yes, this is for me, in this
book I will find the others. Maybe, I will find people like me, and
their words will mirror my experiences and resonate with some
of the truths of being other, ticking other, and being part of the
'tribeless tribe'. It's OK. This is something we all do. We look for
our reflections in the world, we look for our kin, our kind, our
kindred spirits. We are listening for a familiar song in the world.
We look for our story to be represented in television and film, in
poetry and books, in music and art. Being outsider, we don't often
get these narratives seen or heard. Other stories are often hidden
in the noise, obscured in the shadows and underground. Often
Others don't get to take the lead, or the limelight, the glossy front
page, the headline slot, or claim their own space, a place that is for
others to be Other. This is a brave life. It is a bold act, an act of
courage, to put yourself forward to be yourself, to be the shape you
are, to be true to you. You don't have a choice, really, you cannot be
anyone else but you. You are not with the others, and if you're not

with the others, you are Other, outside of here and there, but also somehow inside the outside.

The American psychologist and writer Timothy Leary said:

'Everyone carries a piece of the puzzle. Nobody comes into your life by mere coincidence. Trust your instincts. Do the unexpected. Find the others.'

I love the sentiment in this. I believe that everyone carries a piece of the puzzle. That we are all part of a jigsaw puzzle, that we are all so valuable and a part of a bigger picture. Furthermore what a beautiful and unusual thing it is to find a person that is a jigsaw puzzle piece that kinda fits in the same corner as you. Finding the others and seeking a sense of belonging has been a constant thread through my work as a poet and writer. I question coincidences and see serendipity as a sign that I am on the right road. I hope to continue being able to see and not just look, to be able to seek out and enjoy the magic connections you find when you challenge and push yourself and your work. It's all about learning and growing. If we stop learning and growing we are not alive or present. We need to hear from all perspectives, voices and life stories to get a sense of the bigger picture, even the parts we are not comfortable with.

With all of this in the front of my mind, I write this and tread carefully. I write this remembering that the reader of this particular piece may be other, but may be another Other from me. The reader here may feel differently from me, isolated or alienated in other ways, angry or passionate about other inequalities, but I feel that we connect because of these inequalities and together we identify as being outsider. Now more than ever we have common enemies: intolerance and apathy, ignorance and fear.

I imagine you now and though you may be sitting at a completely different table to me in this world cafeteria, I know you are there and you know I am here. And though we eat our different lunches separately, this knowing, that we are both outside, both eating lunch alone, this will always be our great connection. You and I, we have somehow learned to belong in the unbelonging. So now I hope I have tied an invisible string from your table to mine, I hope this will be no different from all my other writing, writing that hopes to reach outsiders, writing that hopes to explore the what-about-me and to navigate these feelings of isolation. Writing intended to lengthen the table and to add more seats. Writing that I hope can be used as a bridge, to reach other others, to find the others.

My sister Jo-Ann is the most other-Other I know.

She was born with Williams Syndrome. It is a relatively rare developmental disorder which means she has moderate learning difficulties. Jo was born with a number of missing genes on chromosome 7. There is more to her than this. There is more to her than a diagnosis, and I can never hope to fully capture her energy and joy, but here I hope to try. Lately Jo tells us she self-identifies as gay. She is adamant about this identification and so we respect it and accept it. Basically Jo likes girls best. Jo is dual or mixed heritage, Jamaican-Irish and born in the UK. She lives for the big fun, colour and music, to laugh and party, dance and sing. She is like a magpie to shiny things, gold rings, pearls and glitter. She will happily sit for many hours with a pen and a jewellery catalogue ticking her favourite photographs of diamonds and pearls. Just like a child she loves sugar and ice cream, cakes and sweets – her favourites are chocolate caramels and sticky toffee pudding. My sister Jo cannot read or write. I have asked her if she minds me writing about her and she says she's excited about it. She wants us to have a party and to meet you all. She wants you to know about Williams Syndrome. She told me she has some things she wants to tell you all about her life, about being 'special needs' and about her experience of being Other. She believes that people like her have so much they can teach 'normal' children and regular adults too.

I think the language we use for such a rare condition as Williams Syndrome is limited and limiting. Nobody has really heard of Williams Syndrome, so when we use the term to describe Jo, say to a stranger, a cab driver, a waiter in a restaurant, it is met with a blank expression; the listener is none the wiser and cannot help us. But when we use the term 'autistic spectrum' the listener nods and listens more, and if necessary can act and help Jo quicker.[1]

Jo uses the word 'autistic' as her umbrella term to mean herself, her special needs and Williams Syndrome. I think 'special needs' is an inadequate phrase. It is a bit of a lazy blanket expression used to describe a myriad of traits and diagnoses, sometimes painful and/or debilitating, physical and intellectual and emotional. So Jo has adopted the word 'autism' to describe herself. This phrase 'the autistic spectrum' is her shorthand, it is more easily and quickly understood, more visible and mainstream. Many of us have heard of autism; this phrase is used frequently on television, in films and on soaps.

Salena: Do you remember being a little girl?

Jo: Yeah, I was ill most of the time, asthma attacks and eczema... and then they discovered I had Williams Syndrome.

Salena: How does it make you feel to have Williams Syndrome?

Jo: Angry.

Salena: Why?

Jo: Because I want to be like you and I can't and it's frustrating for me and it makes me sad.

Salena (hugs): Ahh, Jo, you're so inspiring and lovely... Do you remember earlier you were talking to me and you told me autistic people can teach other children, can you tell me a bit about that?

Jo: When you're autistic, people don't understand, autistic people don't know how to cope with it, and then they get frustrated... frustration is the thing with autistic children. It's really, really hard. They are trapped! They cannot say what they want to say. Nobody is listening. They are trapped. Trapped.

Salena: Trapped. What's trapping them?

Jo (eye roll and takes a deep intake of breath): You know. Talking. Communication. Umm, what else. Needing the toilet. Reading. Food. They are trapped. And then that's why they get all fired up. Frustrated. They get fired up and want to give up and go home. They cannot cope. Trapped. They are trapped.

Salena: How do you feel now, now you are too big to go to school? What is there for you?

Jo (long pause): Nowhere, there's nothing for me. Once you finish school... You're stuck. I've got no friends out there and it's really sad. I feel like my mum is not doing her art any more because she has to look after me every day. And I've got nobody to come take me out every day and visit me and I am lonely sometimes.

Salena: What do you think people think when they do meet you?

Jo: They probably just want to run away.

Salena: Ahhh, Jo, that's not true…

Jo: But when you go to the shops… people look at you, like weird.

Salena: Tell me what it's like when you go to the shops.

Jo: When I go to the shops people judge… they stare and say 'who is she?' So I've got to cope with that… some nasty people out there.

Salena: What's the one thing you really want?

Jo: A cure.

Salena (hugs): OK, let's switch, do you want to ask me a question?

Jo: Do you think God understands what I am going through every day?

Salena: What do you think, Jo?

Jo: I think God has lots and lots of people running around him and I've just got my mum.

So let's imagine being Jo:

She is thirty-six. She has never left home. My mother has had to be all things – mum and dad, nurse and carer. Jo has never stolen or hurt anyone or killed anything, animal or insect. She hasn't broken any promises. She cannot drive a car or ride a bike. She has no credit cards or debts, no vices or addictions. She is relatively free from the gritty reality of world news, war and terror. However, she does watch the news on TV, and she is aware of some politics, of inequality, her human rights being stripped, of the gay rights movement, the black rights movement, and the cuts to benefits and the NHS. Jo loves nurses. Our grandmothers were nurses. Jo is often in and out of hospital or at doctor's appointments for tests and check-ups. She loves programmes like *Holby City*.

She owns an iPad now and has mastered how to scroll through YouTube to watch her favourite pop stars: Pink, Natalie Imbruglia, Britney Spears, Boy George, Rita Ora, Garbage and Queen. She has learned to FaceTime me and does so whenever she likes, usually at tea-time and on most days. She never looks into the screen properly, so most of my conversations with Jo on FaceTime are to her head and her curly hair. She does not know how to keep a secret. If I were to take her shopping for a birthday gift for Mum, she cannot bear to keep the secret of where the treats are hidden and stands by the cupboard, laughing and singing 'I'm not telling you, Mummy, it's a surprise, it's a surprise,' pointing at the cupboard and laughing, bursting to tell. Imagine not having the tools and the capacity to be secretive, deceptive or evil. Jo dreams of angels and fairies; some mornings she comes downstairs and when you ask her how she slept, she'll shake her head and reply:

'Oh the naughty fairies… they kept waking me up… partying all night!'

My sister Jo was born one cold and grey day in February 1981. I was nine years old when she was born and I loved her and loved having a real live baby doll in the house. She was premature, and so small when she was born, she was smaller than my Tiny Tears doll, I remember measuring them side by side. We didn't know she had Williams Syndrome at first but just that she was fragile, a weak and sickly child. She started having asthma attacks and we didn't know what they were or what to do at first. I shared a room with my mother and my sister in those days, and we'd wait for the doctor to visit with an electric kettle boiling away to make the room humid and steamy, which seemed to help her breathe. We lived in Hastings then, on Springfield Road, in a draughty old house that had never had central heating. It was a terribly worrying time; we didn't know what to do with Jo, but the instinct was to keep her warm and wrapped up at all times. Jo was thin and a fussy eater, she hardly ate. We took photos of her eating, I remember doing this, we were so happy when she ate an actual meal. She was slow to learn to speak, she used baby language for years and communicated with just the odd singular word. At age four or five we were yet to hear a whole sentence from Jo but she loved me to take her to Alexandra Park to feed the ducks and play. I would come home from school and be commanded with 'Park! Nena!' For years I was Nena.

Jo went to a special school. She was learning to cook, they tried to teach her to count, her alphabet to read and write, and she did pottery. By age nineteen, though, that was all finished, all resources and care and respite seemed to dissolve. She is home all day every day now. Mum managed to get Jo some odd days' work experience, maybe an afternoon a week helping at an Oxfam or in the local pet shop. However these opportunities are often fleeting, because they tell us it *isn't feasible*, or because of *insurance*. Always something, a new rule or change of heart closes the door, and this can knock the confidence. Even if the only thing for Jo to do would be to help feed the fish in the pet store, she would be proud of that one responsibility, she'd look forward to it and take pride in it and tell me all about it each week. She loves children and animals and when I ask her what job she would like to do she says she would like to work with the wheelchair children – Jo's name for those she sees as less able than her, children who need her help to sit up and to eat. When I ask her what job she would do if she didn't have special needs, without hesitation she says *nurse*.

It's important that we see ourselves, our stories, our experiences, on the screen and in books, and for me that was perhaps the film *What's Eating Gilbert Grape?* In this movie I see myself as Johnny Depp (Gilbert Grape) and my sister Jo as Leonardo DiCaprio playing Arnie, his brother with learning difficulties. I related to that movie, and most vividly the scene when Gilbert Grape leaves Arnie in the bath. We see Arnie shivering in the bath, still there shivering many hours later as he has been left unattended. And so it is with Jo: you have to plan every moment, or Jo will sit there, anxious and unsure what is happening next. She needs to know step by step each activity. The dialogue at bath time goes: Good girl. Now get out of the bath. That's right. Get dried. Good girl. You are a big girl now, you can do this part, what's next? That's it. Your vest. Good girl. Have you remembered your clean socks?

Just as Arnie does in this movie, my sister Jo really might sit in the bath all day waiting for you to give the next direction or instruction. It is a full-time job caring for her. She might step out in front of a bus, she might wander off with strangers, she could forget the kettle is hot and burn herself, she might get lost in a crowd. I have discovered that this is also a strong Williams Syndrome trait. A need to know what's next in the immediate future and the next exciting things to look forward to, the next party, birthday, Christmas, the next gathering of people and special occasion.

Jo needs a routine, structure; without this she has great anxiety and is likely to have panic attacks. Jo suffers from seizures and spasms, anxiety attacks. I will be talking to her and having an ice cream and then suddenly it is as though she leaves me. At first it looks like she has stopped breathing properly. Then she shakes and vibrates and her eyes roll and go out of focus, she leaves for a few minutes, fitting, convulsing, shaking, spasming, rigid, gasping for breath, then she goes limp and needs a cuddle and she falls asleep for one or two minutes. Just as suddenly she returns, she sits upright again and smiles and she is back in the room as though nothing happened and she picks up her spoon and finishes her ice cream. These spasms hurt her, she says, inside her muscles, where she has clenched up. She can have any number of fits during a day, sometimes none, sometimes five during a Sunday lunch. We still don't really know what triggers them, they seem to come out of nowhere. Is it emotional, anxiety or overexcitement? Or is it connected to diet, like a sugar rush after a Coca-Cola? We still don't know and we are on a waiting list for her to have more neurology tests and the results of a brain scan.

I remember now that I once saw pictures of brain scans, colourful alien images, showing the brain activity of a person with Williams Syndrome as very active and lit up compared to a 'normal' brain, which was mostly grey with the odd flicker of colour. The

Williams Syndrome brain was almost identical to that of someone who had been administered LSD. The LSD brain and the Williams Syndrome brain were vibrant, colourful as a sky on fireworks night, a blaze of colour and lights and connections compared to the dull grey picture of the 'normal' brain. It wouldn't surprise me if all that brain activity is what causes my sister such high emotional euphoria and also chronic emotional exhaustion.

Jo-Ann dreams of going to festivals like her big sister. Every summer she sees me coming and going, tents and wellies, rain and mud, and every summer she wants to come with me. She also wants to go to Gay Pride, she wants to go clubbing, she wants to go and see bands play live, like any big music lover does. We know she couldn't cope with the crowds. We worry for her, worry that the heat and anxieties and crowds would overwhelm her, that she would have fits and panic attacks. Another trait of Williams Syndrome is a high sensitivity to noises and volume.

So, this year for her birthday we turned our house into a festival and called it JOMAD. The main stage was in the lounge, friends showed up with guitars and played live music. There was VIP camping in our dining room – we'd put up her tent and filled it with cushions and pillows. Our kitchen was the backstage bar. A feast of prettiest pink fairy cakes and caramel chocolate bars. Our bathroom the portaloo and in our garden we had a bonfire. I invited my friends, poets and artists and musicians, and asked them to all come dressed as though they were going to be at Pride or Glastonbury, so they all appeared wearing rainbows and wigs and wellies. We had a guest list and wristbands at the door. Glitter got everywhere. Jo got up and sang Amy Winehouse's 'Back to Black' with the girls and knew all the words. It was the best day of the year. We love Jo's birthdays. It was a great joy to see how very, very happy she was that day. Her joy is infectious, she makes everyone have a laugh, she makes people around her want to be happy, playful, dancing, lively.

Every birthday we ask Jo to check the postbox and as usual she finds dozens of birthday cards from all her friends: Kylie, Pink, Mariah Carey, Madonna, Beyoncé, Robbie Williams, Leonardo DiCaprio, Keanu Reeves... She truly believes these people know of her and remember her birthday every year. She tears into the envelopes and we read the cards out to her and she laughs and laughs and claps her hands. That Mark Owen from Take That, he keeps writing to her every birthday every single year all her life. Oh Mark! She swoons. He loves me, doesn't he.

Eventually it's bedtime and we try to get her into the tent we set up for her in the dining room and we tell her it is lovely and cosy in there. But no, she's not having any of it.

'But if we were at a festival you'd have to sleep in a tent...'

I try and coax her in.

'No way! I'll sleep in a real bed upstairs... thank you very much!'

I love my sister Jo, I adore her, everybody does. My mother is in her early seventies now and I know a day will come soon when my partner Richard and I may have to take the reins and be my sister's carers. It will be a full-time job. I have no idea how my mother manages it every day; her constant love, patience and devotion are remarkable. Everyone who meets Jo loves her; she's the life and soul of every occasion. But as child-like, pixie-like as she may seem, she is a thirty-six-year-old woman now and is justified in being frustrated and angry sometimes. Jo will speak her mind. She will let you know clearly when she feels patronised and how she feels about things she won't eat or sounds or smells that upset her. All of her senses are sharper and more finely tuned than mine. In public her sudden comments or outbursts, her fits, her rocking back and forth, her anxious rubbing of her hands, her need for cuddles and connection, her petting of dogs and her displays of affection, vocal and physical, can be unsettling for strangers. She cannot suppress herself or her impulses in the same way we can. When she was a little kid it looked 'normal' for her to run across a restaurant to pet a puppy, but it looks odd now to some. In clothes shops she runs up to dresses and touches them and cries out with pleasure, stroking them, because the fabric is soft and silky. When I invite her to my poetry gigs, she has such confidence, and has leaped up on stage and belted out 'We Are the Champions' by Queen. The crowd joins in and everyone applauds her. 'We Are the Champions' has become Jo's theme tune in London poetry circles. However, some 'normal' people just see the surface, they see someone making a noise and a fuss, they see a blatant show of emotion, a loud expression of love and joy, so often I see my sister frowned upon, stared or tutted at, or seen as anti-social by the miserable and the judgemental and the 'normal' in society.

My empathy and solidarity with my sister and with others is part of my life. I will continue to speak up and march for others, for all of our human rights. I always felt that, if they can take one of us down, then they can come for all of us. We are all more connected than we realise, and more similar. Now more than ever, now in this era of performative cruelty, it is our differences that unite us. And our actions of kindness and tolerance are more vital than ever. We must all stand up and speak up, take room and make room for all other others.

I believe strongly that once an idea or a notion is heard it cannot be unheard. So please keep going and never give up, keep talking, keep marching, keep organising, keep writing and keep sharing. Speak up for the people who perhaps cannot vote, who cannot march, who cannot be heard, the people who need our NHS more than we do. The people who need assistance, support, funding, care and our humanity.

There is no such thing as the voiceless, we all have voices. We just sing an Other tune. We are like birds, we all sing, but there is the one 'normal' bird song that is constantly amplified, and all the other birds are muted, ignored, clipped, caged or shot down. So share your songs and help and amplify the Others to sing louder!

Salena: Mum, is there anything you want to add?

Lorna: It's been an adventure for me being a parent of a child with complex symptoms. It's complicated, frustrating, sometimes it stretches one's patience to the limits. It is frustrating in that you are educating people as you go along in life because Williams Syndrome is not well known, I mean, from doctors to dentists to people you meet in the street, even your closest friends. This person depends on you totally, so most of your life is put aside. It's not all doom and gloom, it's rewarding and funny being Jo's mum, we have a lot of laughs, don't we... humour is so important, and it makes up for everything that we both have had to endure. The earlier you can get a diagnosis the better. My advice for anyone who has a child diagnosed with Williams Syndrome is it's all about listening. Keep things simple and be clear about plans. Here is a child with a low pain threshold, with an acute sense of smell and taste and hearing, and a big heart and empathy. If you are lucky enough to have a child with Williams Syndrome find out and nurture what they love and are passionate about – in Jo's case music, she loves her music, we have music playing in the house all the time.

Salena: And can we have one last word from you, Jo? Is there anything you want people to know?

Jo: I want people to know I am happy being me. I get sad sometimes because people stare and they don't understand how that makes me feel. I'm like you, I like baking, I like eating, I like parties, I like kittens and puppies, I like to have fun. I am not that different. I don't like people being impatient, I don't like prejudice… See you at the party, everybody! We are the champions!

A Short Story

Tom Shakespeare

I feel me. I really do. I don't feel Other. I believe without thinking that I am just like everyone else. Like all of you. I may look out through these distinctive green eyes, but I think with this normal brain. I speak, the same. Hear, the same. Feel, the same.

How wrong I am! I don't look the same. I have always been obviously different. From infancy, I grew up, or didn't grow up, like this. So shortness of stature, this restriction of growth, this, say it, *dwarfism*, has always been my ordinary. I can't help it, I can't escape it. This is who I am. It's all I've ever known. I always forget the most unusual thing about me. It's certainly the first thing you're aware of. But I'm often as surprised as you.

Perhaps it's because, for most of my life, I have been barely limited by this disability. Maybe I couldn't walk so far or stand so long, but really, it's a small difference, between friends. I can manage almost everything, and no allowances are required, expected or asked for. I do struggle to change the duvet, it's true. I used to clamber up, or stand on a stool to get things down. But I would far rather no fuss was made; nothing much is required for me to adapt. Extend the pedals on my car. Reach down something for me, please.

I am always surprised by the reactions of Others. Who are they staring at? Why do they jump out of their skin when they see me suddenly, standing at the door or framed in the lift when it opens? Is it me they are looking at? Is it me they think is different? What do they find so odd? Why do they urge my difference upon me? Do they not realise that I am in almost every respect exactly the same as them, no more, not much less, however unusual my seeming might appear?

To me, my stature is a small thing. To them, it is everything.

A moment: I am acting in a play at school. It is *The Insect Play* by the brothers Capek, an opportunity to get dozens of kids on stage together, all the ants and butterflies and beetles. I get into my costume, a boiler suit, and my face is made up in garish fashion, my hair gelled. I look at my fifteen-year-old self in the dressing room mirror and say: 'My own mother would not recognise me.' Everyone around me guffaws. It takes me a moment or two to realise how silly my comment was. Of course my mother will recognise me on stage. There is no one else in the cast who is a dwarf. There is no one else in the whole school who is a dwarf. I am always the odd one out. I keep on forgetting that I'm not like the Others. I'm never one of the crowd, however desperately I want to be.

My most critical task in life is to manage the interaction that is strained by my unusual appearance, to put the Others at their ease. It doesn't usually take very long. My true friends do not seem to notice, after a while. Most of us people with restricted growth, all dwarfs who make a success out of life, are the same.

Humour helps. We make a joke about our difference. Small person, large personality. We play the life and soul, and the Others feel relaxed. Now the Others don't have to worry, because plainly we don't need worrying about. They don't have to be concerned about saying the wrong thing. We can take a joke, after all we have to. If you can't beat them, join them.

But mostly, I don't want you to draw attention to it. I want you to join with me to ignore it. I am willing you not to say anything. To overlook my little difference. Collusion? Denial? Or getting on with the uncontroversial? That's why I hate it when people make a fuss. Don't mention it, please. When I was a teenager, my mother said once, looking at my clothes: it's bad enough that you are small, you mustn't draw attention to yourself… by which she meant, draw attention by being scruffy or having earrings or being a punk. When she visited me at school or at college, she would always do her best to straighten me out. Fixing my tie, or tucking in my shirt for me. Brushing my hair – when I had any. How excruciating for an adult, to be not quite right. Later, she would throw up her hands in despair: 'Oh, Thomas!'

The correct answer, the one she always hoped for, was that I would be conventional, like my dad, three-piece-suit every day to the surgery, a sports jacket at weekends, no different to any other suburban male GP in England. But I never wanted to join that uniformed establishment, even if it would have had me. It was worth the occasional humiliation to be the different person who felt right, out on left field. I wanted to fade into the background of another clan, a more rebellious conformity. I would become a different sort of doctor.

Another moment: I am invited to a drinks party with the Archbishop of Canterbury at Lambeth Palace. There is a whole crowd of us that evening. Writers. Artists. Scientists. Several members of Monty Python. The Children's Laureate. Famous sceptics and famous believers. And others of us, less distinguished, wondering why we are in such exalted company. To this day, I'm not clear about the reason for the invitation. Maybe it's something to do with the diversity of England. The prelate with the people.

The Archbishop slowly does the social rounds, his wine in hand. He reaches us, and then immediately kneels on the floor in front of me for a few moments' chat. I am mortified. He's drawing attention to me. Everyone is around us, aware of him, us. People might be staring. It's not necessary for him to kneel. I am not worthy. He must be in pain. He looks uncomfortable down there. Although kneeling, presumably, is what he does every day. And he does it solemnly, seriously. I admire him. I try to talk about one of his devotional books which I have enjoyed. He is the primate of the Church of England, the most senior person in the kingdom outside of the Royal Family. It's not right that he comes down to my level. But it's not about status, this gesture of acceptance and inclusion. He creaks to his feet again, smiles, continues. He's a good man.

Whoever they are, however kind, however thoughtful, I always want to say to people: Get up! Please! Don't squat or crouch or kneel. It looks painful, you wobble, we two make a fine sight. Don't make a fuss. If it's hard for you to crane your neck downwards, we could sit together on chairs, so we are at the same height. Don't draw attention to my difference, please.

If you want to kiss me, wonderful. Thank you. That's acceptance, the connection I was hoping for. Let's sit down on this sofa, it'll be easier. Let's even lie down on this bed. There now, that's more comfortable. Particularly with our shoes off. Stretched out flat, we actually fit quite well. Our height difference isn't such an issue when we're horizontal. We're on the level. Our faces are the same, human faces. See, we can lie together cheek to cheek, and you don't have to get neck-ache. After ten minutes you will barely notice that my toes are not exactly entwined with yours. We could share a bath later. There are advantages. The difference wears off, after a while.

Although I must warn you, when we go out together, everyone will stare. You'll get used to it. You now have honorary membership in the clan; however tall you are, they're wondering about you now.

But I admit that my friends, all of them, seem to get used to me and us and my difference becomes unremarkable, no odder than her glasses and his sore hip and all the other worn-out body parts and rebellious metabolisms that ageing people suffer from. The thousand natural shocks that flesh is heir to, as Hamlet would have it.

So. The Others. You want to know more about the Others.

The Others stare at me. Every day, everywhere. Their children laugh, and point, and gather round. The children talk excitedly to each other, ask the same questions over and over again. I avoid the times that schools come out, I dread the crocodile on the street, the wearisome exposure to eyes that may not know any better but still scorch me.

There are always children in supermarkets, I can hear them as I pass.

Is that a child or a man?

Is that a little mummy or a little daddy?

Why is he so small?

Why does he have a big head?

How old is he?

How can he be big if he is little?

There's a funny man, a silly man, a little man…

Look, look, look, quick, quick, quick.

Parents never know how to react. Sometimes they ignore the child. Sometimes they smack the child. They bark in shame: 'Don't stare!' or 'I've told you, it's rude to stare!' Sometimes they just glance at me and look away, mortified, wishing the ground would swallow them up. Or swallow me up.

I befriend every child I can. I smile at them. I play peek-a-boo. I wave. I tell them I am just different, there's nothing to worry about. I answer their questions. I tell them tall stories, with a wink. They're not difficult to handle, when there's only one or two of them. I want them to go away reassured. There's nothing to see here, no need for concern, I am just like them, or rather, just like their dad.

My own dad was a doctor, a paediatrician. He chose to work with children. I've seen his white coat, made especially for him. I've heard stories that, back in the children's ward, the patients used to jump up and down on their beds: 'We want our little doctor! We want our little doctor!'

I remember the Geordie lads, wheeling their guy for pennies one November. They stared at me curiously as I passed on my way to the shops. Returning, I found them with the courage to question me:

'Mister, mister, do you smoke?' When, then, I had to admit I did, they continued on their way satisfied, leaving me mystified. Until I realised that a teacher or parent must have previously warned them: smoking stunts your growth. Not an independent, hard-working adult then, but a walking health promotion advertisement.

Being small is not something you get over. You may not wake up every morning feeling different, but you are reminded every time you leave the house. Children may not know any better, but adults do. Particularly after a few drinks, they act worse. I've overheard them in the bar, in the train buffet, on the street. I've heard the names they call me. The words they call out, call me to my face:

I'm a midget, a half-pint, a Mekon, a Munchkin, an Oompa-Loompa, Mini Me, Wee Man. I'm a goblin, a blob, a short-arse. A freak.

The Others now have mobile phone cameras. They stop and take my photograph to pass around later in the pub and laugh about. Mocking me strengthens them.

A moment. To my surprise, as I am walking home, a car suddenly screeches to a halt on the street, reverses, a man jumps out, runs round, crouches, fires off his camera, runs back to his pal in the car howling with laughter.

As soon as inhibitions dissolve, people like me become fair game. Avoid the pubs at closing time, whatever you do. Steer clear of gangs of inebriated young people. Don't let them pick you up, push you around, throw you down like a human skittle.

A moment. I am on the Tyne and Wear Metro, going home one evening, sitting by myself on the train. I have my laptop in my bag, I have come from the office, from being an important academic. A gang of teenage girls, high on pills or cheap alcohol, gather round me, start harassing me, won't go away. Humiliating, nasty, mean and vicious questions, probing, mocking, abusing. Nobody on the train seems to notice or care what is happening, in real time, as the Metro chugs south over the river. I am worried about what will happen when it's time for me to get up. Will they snatch my bag? The girl gaggle follow me off the train, get bored, dash away. Relief. But twenty minutes that leave me shaken.

Twenty minutes which explain why some people who have restricted growth would never go on public transport, would never expose themselves to the Others. They stick to the protective bubble of their private car, or never go out at all. They know they are vulnerable to the stares, the shoves, the words and worse.

Being a dwarf isn't a big problem. It's not a degenerative illness. You don't drown in a lungful of phlegm, your muscles don't waste away, your skin doesn't fall off, you don't eat your own fingers. Having restricted growth doesn't affect the brain. It doesn't stop you leading a normal life, it doesn't stop you getting it up. Dwarfism is at the easy end of the spectrum of disability, the place where physical difference becomes just another variation, not a heartbreaking medical tragedy.

But the Others, they make it a problem. I don't want to think about the Others.

They're not always rude. Sometimes it's the tyranny of cute that takes over.

They tell me I'm sweet, I'm brave, I'm special, I'm amazing, I'm unforgettable, they know someone just like me, I'm related to every other dwarf in the world, of course I must know them. We all look just the same. They've met me before, no they definitely have, didn't I use to work in the DHSS? They don't mean to be funny, but...

They're doing their best to reach out to me, but it's not working. Who are they looking at? All they can see is what I never notice and don't want to be stereotyped as. They're not seeing real me at all, because they can't see beyond this head, that body.

Because whether I'm a comedy or a tragedy, a caution or an inspiration, I'm never just a private person, a man who signifies nothing, only a face in the crowd.

Except perhaps somewhere where we're all different, a gathering of people like me. For a few minutes it feels odder than odd, and then I feel at home, with my own, where everyone understands and it doesn't matter any more. But those are rare moments, when we outnumber the Others and they realise that nobody stages *Snow White* in summertime and so we must be the new normal in town.

Or these last years, now that I mostly use a wheelchair, I have discovered the secret of invisibility. Nothing remarkable about a disabled on wheels. Look past, nothing to notice, fewer stares (don't talk about the stairs).

Perhaps that's why I have made radio my home, that place where you are a voice only, ideas first, in your head but not in your face, where I am no less and no more than any other.

Out of that box, on a good day, I'm Tyrion Lannister, fortified and full of advice:

'Never forget what you are. The rest of the world will not. Wear it like armour, and it can never be used to hurt you.'

But the stock of pride can go down as well as up. Sticks and stones can hurt, and so do words, on a bad day. C. P. Cavafy, another outsider, wrote of the seventh-century Alexandrian Aemilianus Monae:

> With my words, my image and my manners
> I'll make an armored vestment truly sound
> That will guard me from evil schemers,
> And every weakness, every fear confound.

Sword and sorcery dwarfs, pointy hat dwarfs, from J. R. R. Tolkien and C. S. Lewis, got me through an adolescence when I wanted to fit in, to hide my wounds, to find respect, to get the girl. Later, I went to Cambridge University to study Anglo-Saxon, Norse and Celtic, the deep tradition of stories and sagas that Tolkien and Lewis knew intimately and drew on.

Why did you choose that course, people still ask me, when you are such a man of now, of social change and disability rights?

I think because they spoke to me then, and do still, the old stories that still resonate, of goblins and elves, changelings and dwarfs, where there is a place for everyone, however misshapen, where we are all special, where we might even have magic powers of which you know nothing. (As long as you're a male. It's a rule. Elves and fairies can be female, but never dwarfs or goblins.) Where green eyes help.

Because being yourself is tough, in a world without dragons.

The Other Side of Gender

Rachel Mann

'You're like a Jewish person who wants to join the Nazi Party.' A close friend said that to me twenty-odd years ago when I told him I'd become a Christian and was going to start going to church. Undoubtedly, his rhetoric was inflated, questionable and, arguably, tasteless. Yet, as far as he could see it had grip. For I am a trans woman, and he reckoned my desire to join a church was indicative of either a form of self-loathing (which one might now call 'internalised transphobia') or a symptom of a degree of recklessness bordering on masochism or a breakdown. He thought that Christians – especially the evangelical Christians I planned to start worshipping with – would love my sincere faith, but hate (even persecute) my gender expression and sexual identity. And, if his comparison with Nazi persecution of Jewish people is over the top, he was convinced I was placing myself in a situation that could only lead to psychological and emotional trauma. I would be entering a culture that meant death: for my queerness and otherness, and – in the face of potentially relentless bullying and gaslighting – perhaps the death of my own body.

In recent years, for trans people in countries like the United Kingdom, things have arguably got better. We've had, as the media sometimes puts it, 'a bit of a moment'. Whereas for my generation the nearest we got to icons and role models were drawn from the pages of tabloid exposés, in the twenty-first century one readily finds high-profile trans actors, writers, artists, politicians and legislators. The internet and social media supply links and networks which enable trans and gender non-conforming people to create unprecedented support networks and organise and stand in solidarity together. Large campaigning organisations like Stonewall which, for decades, treated trans people as the embarrassing other of queer rights have brought trans identities centre-stage.

And yet… in so many respects transgender people remain icons of otherness. The English language is littered with words which, for trans people, signal 'other'. These words sometimes turn into nettles and barbed wire in our mouths; sometimes, in the voices of our opponents, they become weapons against us. I am not talking so much about the obvious slurs, though one might include those too. I think I've been called all of them over the years. Slur terms like 'HeShe' or 'SheMale' exist to fetishize, punish, control and mock persons whose bodies don't conform to normative ideas. They are powerful means of othering.

No, I am more interested in the slipperiness of the language used by and applied to trans people, even when we – trans people – hope it does some positive, creative good. Once upon a time, I was inclined to refer to myself as 'transsexual', that is, as someone who, through hormones, surgery and social identity, has sought to make their body as congruent as possible with their gender identity. I've not entirely abandoned the term. However, I'm conscious of the extent to which it is a loaded, medicalised expression. 'Transsexuals' represent a relatively niche part of the trans spectrum, and yet we've sometimes been taken as a kind of norm for trans identities. In a time when the trans community has become more confident about its wild and delicious diversity, trans people themselves have become strong critics of the idea that 'proper' trans people are people like me, the ones who give themselves over to the ministrations of the medical and psychiatric profession.

So, words and phrases that get used by both trans and non-trans people sometimes seem simultaneously helpful, yet insufficient to hold the weight of emerging narratives and identities. We think they look strong, then they break. Another classic example is that tabloidy phrase I struggle with: 'woman trapped inside a man's body' (or 'man trapped' etc.). It's one of those phrases that's been around for decades and originated in writings about male homosexuality in the nineteenth century. Many trans people disavow it. I've heard others use it positively. At best, it's flimsy metaphor; at worst, it creates pictures of trans lives that limit, parody and other. It's flimsy because it barely begins to capture the complexities of trans people's lived experience (in my own case, I didn't feel like there was a person trapped inside me; it was the whole experience of my body that was distressing). Yet, as a phrase which has caught on in popular discourse, it's meant that some trans people have felt like they should talk about their lives as if there was a person 'trapped inside'. The phrase breaks on our lips and wounds us. Words and phrases like this flag up just how much people like me are others in a world that still privileges cisgender, heterosexual people.[1]

There are other, subtler words which both reveal and limit. They mark out the trickiness of the path I and others have followed. Words like 'stealth' and 'passing'. For anyone unfamiliar with the notions of trans 'stealth' and 'passing', perhaps my own experience of them will help. When I transitioned in the early nineties one of the key requirements from the NHS psychiatrists who 'treated' me – a condition of becoming a recipient of HRT and being recommended for surgery – was undertaking the so-called Real Life Test or Experience. This requirement remains a key, controversial part of NHS treatment. To be recommended for surgery, I needed to demonstrate I'd lived in my transitioned gender for two years and worked for one year of that time too. When I met with my psychiatrists, the litany of questions always included some about how I was seen: did I 'pass', did I think I 'passed', what kind of gaze did I think was directed at me? The imperative, both spoken and unspoken, was (as a male-to-female trans person) 'to pass' as a woman, to achieve invisibility and blend in; that is, to be not seen as trans, but to pass as cisgender. 'Success' – from a psychiatric, medical point of view – was measured by being seen socially and publicly as 'just like' any other cis woman.

Of course, running alongside this was the conservatism of the psychiatrists who were supporting me. Their ideas about what, for example, constituted a woman were of an essentially conventional kind. A woman wears make-up, wears a skirt or dress, is attracted to men and so on. When I visited the Gender Identity Clinic, I learned to 'act up' to their stereotypes – it simply made my life easier and I was more likely to get what I wanted (my hormone prescription, the prospect of surgery) if I 'performed' according to their script. If it wasn't quite the case that I'd turn up for appointments rocking what I called the 'full Laura Ashley' (floral frock, big hair and pink lipstick), I was not far off. On reflection, it was all rather humiliating. I knew what I needed to survive and a small group of powerful male psychiatrists possessed access to it.

Those who disobeyed – because they saw themselves as gender-neutral or genderqueer, or just wouldn't play gender games set by a psychiatrist – were likely to run into trouble. Trans people so often get caught in a lens that makes us 'other'. Simply to survive we can feel we have to live through that lens. I and other trans people have often performed stereotyped femininity/masculinity for the sake of psychiatry. 'Passing' is a narrative of disappearance that's simultaneously controversial and significant for the trans community. For, on the one hand, I – like many trans people – was rather desperate to 'pass' (not least because I so completely wanted to be seen/accepted as a woman); however, on the other, 'passing' can be read as an introjection generated by medical, social and cultural expectations.

'Passing' can easily be connected to an allied concept, 'stealth'. Again, my own experience is illuminating. As I transitioned I was keen to pass and perhaps had certain social advantages – youth, stereotyped 'feminine' physical characteristics, access to money, etc. – to achieve that end. Like many trans people who – on these terms – 'successfully' transition I saw the social and personal advantages of 'going stealth'. That is, effectively excising all reference to my trans identity. I enacted my disappearance into 'ordinary' society by living as if I was a cisgender woman. Letting people know I was trans became the exception rather than the norm.

This practice is sufficiently controversial among trans people that – while it is understood as a practice with a history, and therefore, one might say, part of a trans tradition – it has been seen by some in trans communities as an example of internalised transphobia. In other words, to 'go stealth' is to act as if one is so fearful and anxious about one's status as trans that one seeks to 'pretend' or act as if one is not trans. One thing I'm clear about in my own case is that, 'successful' though my transition was from the point of the view of the dominant psychiatric and social narrative, I was often anxious about being 'spotted' or outed as trans and, thereby, stigmatised or ostracised by those who'd 'spotted' me.

One of the things one learns in any context in which being trans is inescapably 'other' and 'othered' is that there is no escape from cost and loss. There is no safe space. Those who perform or foreground their trans identities face abuse and violence, but those who go stealth live in the terror of discovery and outing. One of the indicators that we live in a cis-normative culture is the prevalence of the narrative that trans people are duplicitous and tricksterish. This has inner and outer dimensions. The inner dimensions can be acute when it comes to forming intimate relationships. I – along with other trans people I've known – have felt pressure to disclose my most intimate personal truths in order to enjoy the kind of everyday relationships many people unconsciously take for granted. The internalised belief that being trans is somehow shameful has led me to the 'there's something you need to know about me' conversation on too many occasions. I've felt like I've been making a dirty confession. Yet the 'outer' dimension – in which men have attacked and killed trans people and offered 's/he tricked me' as a defence – is also well attested.

Perhaps the only fair thing to acknowledge is that such are the pressures on being trans that one must simply do what one must to survive. Sometimes the only option for trans people is to live in an endless negotiation, deciding when to use stealth and when to be out and proud. It's costly and tiresome, but also human and real. At one level, I think it signals the extent to which trans people are simply variants on the ordinary spectrum of identity. For each of us, whether cis or trans, gay or straight, must make negotiations about when we disclose and when to hold back. Cis-het people have certain privileges, for sure, as do those trans people who can pass as cis.[2] However, I sense that all of us hold a deep, abiding otherness and strangeness within ourselves. One doesn't have to be trans to know how toxic cultural, social and religious norms play out in our inner lives. Each of us negotiates for ourselves what social concepts of 'man' or 'woman' or 'being good', or whatever, mean for us. Much of the time these norms do not match our lived experiences. If we are to live well, surely a negotiation of oddness will be unavoidable. None of us, in the end, are terribly normal.

You may be wondering what happened to me when I started going to church. Perhaps the easiest way to sum it up is to say that I became a Church of England priest. This might be taken as a signal that I – as a trans person – was met with open arms by an institution my friend imagined would persecute me. Well, it wasn't that simple. I'd be lying if I said my otherness has not presented challenges from within the Church. At times, I've been the object of serial mocking and spite. The Church is not an easy place in which to be a woman, let alone an out LGBT⁺ person. Yet I have also been cherished by very many. The Church is an odd institution. I know some would be delighted if I were 'defrocked'. Defrocked! Only in an organisation as wondrously strange and other could someone imagine that 'frock-wearing' was the proper business of straight, cis men!

Ironically, the Church has offered an extraordinary space for me to delight in and come to terms with my otherness as a trans person. For, if the Church mostly gets it horribly wrong, at its heart is a desire and call towards reconciliation. And this has implications across every aspect of life – international, national, local and personal. As an internal concept 'Other' so often refers to those aspects and dimensions of our selves we readily write off, are afraid of or wish to bury or destroy. In my teen years, there was simply no doubt that my desire to be female was precisely the kind of dimension of myself that I wanted to wipe away, tried to bury and destroy; yet no matter what strategy I adopted, it came back stronger and more insistently. It was a part of me that sickened me because it seemed abnormal, other and made me different. I saw it as 'wrong' and in need of excision. Perhaps this experience, especially when we're teenagers, is pretty much universal. It is a time when we undergo rapid change, a series of transitions, from childhood to adulthood. It can make us anxious about how others see us and, most especially, how we see ourselves. We can be so insecure that we try to hide those parts of us – our insecurities, sexual inadequacies and so on – from ourselves and others. In one sense, my experience of being trans was just one variant on that; it was simply one way of being human.

Transitioning was a journey into reconciliation and, for me, reconciliation goes deeper than me merely accepting myself as a woman. It's meant re-embracing and loving that within me that I want to disavow: my childhood, my bewildering experience of being socialised 'as a boy'. To open myself up to those things about me that I consider 'male' or 'mannish' has been akin to walking among the dead. It has been a journey into so many things I'd rather forget. It has entailed travelling into darkness. It has been like the work of a cold case pathologist who, when presented with a long dead body, attempts to unlock its secrets.

Yet, there is resurrection too. It has taken me many years of honest and authentic self-reflection to become at peace with the simple, unavoidable fact that some aspects of my past life are dissonant with where and who I am now. For me, the immense and joyous good news has taken the form of a discovery: that such dissonance, paradox and inconsistency is creative, thrilling and risky in the best sense of the word. The 'shalom' in my Self is not of a comforting and easily resolved kind. Yet, there is such a thing as grace. It is what had made it possible for me to embrace the dissonance within and go beyond my places of safety and prejudice. By reconciling that which seems impossible, grace brings new hope. I do not care if you choose to see this grace as the work of God or not. It is real. And within it I have begun to find a way to a place where I both rejoice in who I am and what I have become, and also am glad of and delight in who I was.

A TARDIS OF SOULS

Others

Matt Haig

Life is changing,
That's what they say.
The world is round;
And some humans are gay.

Some people are Other colours,
Some come from Other places
Some believe in Other gods,
Some are made of Other races.

The Others are everywhere;
They're always around.
The Others are screaming;
They just don't make a sound.

I feel in my bones
That life was once great.
And to find that utopia,
I must follow the hate.

The Others are rising,
The press says they're getting stronger
I know I can't take this
For very much longer.

There's so much complexity,
It's too much to understand.
I want to know the world
Like the back of my hand.

I look in the mirror,
And am too scared to see,
That it's my self who has changed;
And the Other is me.

Choosing Sides

Alex Preston

We moved to Kent in 2016, just before the Brexit referendum. The process of finding a home and a school for the kids, the painful practicalities of shifting four lives from London to the countryside; these things absorbed us so much that the vote seemed to creep up almost unnoticed, a sudden sea of red Leave signs springing like early poppies by the side of every road.

We'd lived in a typical London bubble: our neighbours, the parents of our kids' friends at school, the people we ran into at the deli and the pub and the library, they all saw the world through the same eyes as we did. They may have been from Poland or Trinidad or Latvia or Slough, but we enjoyed a kind of sympathetic shortcut with these people, an assumption that we were on the same side in all the big battles. We thought we knew the things we'd miss most when we left London – the food, the theatre, the music. In fact, something quite different opened like a chasm in our lives. We recognised the hidden comfort that came from being surrounded by like-minded people.

This isn't a piece about Brexit. I haven't anything new to say about that. I went to sleep that night of 23 June like all of my friends (and, it transpired, few of my new neighbours) secure in the knowledge that my countrymen and women weren't insane enough to blow up the boat that was ferrying them. I woke to find that someone, in the deep night, had knocked down the VOTE REMAIN sign at the end of my drive. But, as I said, this isn't about Brexit. It's about cricket.

A friend of my mother's had a breakdown when I was five or six. I remember going to visit her. She lived in Surrey, a fact which may or may not have been linked to her fragile mental state. I wasn't sure what I expected to find; at that age, you're still trying out words, knitting a net of language and attempting to throw it over the things you find in the world. Marion wasn't comatose in bed, or raving in a straitjacket. She was just a bit quiet. Now I'm not saying that I was as bad as Marion in the days that followed the referendum, but I found myself confecting reasons to head up to London, calling old friends more often than was healthy, attempting to live without talking to my neighbours, to the workers and shopkeepers of Kent. I felt a quiet desperation fuzzing my vision, waking me early, transforming the minor inconveniences of life into insuperable tribulations. If it wasn't a breakdown, then it was something close.

I'd joined the local cricket club when we came to Kent, a perk I'd held out to myself when we were contemplating the move, one of the foundation visions of the good life we were building for ourselves. The cricket ground is down by the river, and across the road from a decent pub. It's overhung by horse chestnuts whose candles light the first month of every season and backed by high banks of cow parsley and mallow. The team is made up of locals – the vet, the tree surgeon, the son of the groundsman, various agricultural types, a butcher. There were few DFL (Down From London) types like me, but I was guardedly welcomed and played a few games for them with neither great distinction nor abject humiliation.

It was an evening not long after the Brexit vote, the sun still high, the air thick and busy with insects. I'd spent the day locked in my study trying to meet a deadline that had passed some weeks earlier. Coming out into the warmth of the summer evening, with chiffchaffs tinkling in the trees and the zip of sprinklers on lawns, I felt as human as I had for a while. We had a fixture at a sports centre on the outskirts of one of the sad seaside towns that stretch along the coast. I drove down with the windows open. Our opposition were from the town's Bangladeshi community – a collection of stern silver-haired men and their lean sons. I could tell my teammates were nervous as we went onto the field. The balls came fast and true and we were bowled out for something embarrassing like sixty. Then it was the opposition's turn to bat. I wasn't sure who started it, but the jokes seemed to move around the field like dark zephyrs, whispered from one fielder to the next, greeting each player as he came out. There was something almost quaint about it – this was a particularly British kind of racism, dredged up from the 1970s, Alf Garnett in cricket whites. We lost the game, thankfully, but even afterwards, as we changed, the same jokes, the same high and frantic laughter. I went and apologised to the opposition captain and drove home in a rage. I spent that night looking at houses in Kilburn on Primelocation.

A rope was thrown to me from an unlikely source. A friend's mother had heard I was a cricketer. She volunteered at a local reception centre for unaccompanied child migrants who were, at that time, arriving in their hundreds at Kent's port towns from Syria, Afghanistan and Eritrea, via France. The boys – and this place was all boys – were traumatised, bristling with resentment, forced too early into their adult skins. There was an old grey tennis court near the long 'L' of old prefab huts that housed the boys. When I first visited the centre an invisible division had been drawn along the line of the absent net. On one side the Syrians and Eritreans kicked a scuffed football across the concrete; on the other, the Afghan boys had constructed a set of stumps out of three sticks bound together with a shoelace, and were playing cricket with a tennis ball and a child's bat.

A few days later, with the help of the genial and portly Nigerian security guard who manned the door at the centre, we turned the field behind the dining hall into a makeshift cricket pitch. From then on, my Wednesday afternoons were spent with Hafez, Ali, Abdul-Ghani and Kabir, our games augmented by curious Syrians and Eritreans, or Afghans who stayed only a few days as they were transported north to meet family or friends already resident. Abdul-Ghani had represented his country at Under-18 level and, a head and a half taller than me, he bowled with a kind of liquid grace, the ball fizzing and spitting in the air before exploding off the rough earth of our hastily rolled wicket. Kabir was small and wily, a spin bowler and comedian who grinned disquietingly as he batted.

We'd found some cricket equipment in a cupboard at the centre. I had over the years accumulated more bats and helmets than I'd ever have use for. I started off trying to coach the boys, calling to mind the fierce cricket master at school who'd done his best to knock the love of the game out of me; soon, though, it became clear that I was the least gifted player amongst us, and so we enjoyed long games of four- or five-a-side, the security guard joining in and proving himself a useful slip fielder. Hafez was the best batsman, a punchy, quick-footed player and the only one who could deal with Abdul-Ghani's yorkers. Ali, who was the youngest of the four, had faced Abdul-Ghani without a helmet and wore his black eye with pride. I'd been told not to ask questions about their lives back in Afghanistan, but we spent enough time together that eventually I knew a good deal about the horror and the haunted nights; the disappearances of loved ones; the frustrated ambitions of these quiet, decent, intelligent boys.

Those Wednesday afternoons stretched into evenings, and often we'd play for four or five hours straight, pausing only to drink from a shared water bottle or to talk about our favourite players – Dhoni, Shahzad, Kohli, Zadran. The weather was always kind to us and the wicket, which the Nigerian guard rolled most evenings, was beginning to play true. The boys invited me to celebrate Eid with them and we ate pastries and danced to Egyptian music and tried to persuade the Syrians of the superiority of cricket to football. The reception centre – with its austere and institutional atmosphere, its harried but well-meaning staff, its situation in a system that sought to make it as difficult as possible for boys like this to find shelter in the UK – nonetheless became a place of solace, even of joy for these boys, with cricket the glue that bound them together.

Naturally, the fact that I only came to supervise them on Wednesdays didn't stop the boys from playing every other day of the week, and I could see them improving as they put muscle on their skinny bones, as they ironed the errors out of their game. I realised that they needed somewhere less ramshackle to practise and, knowing that nobody used the nets at my local ground on a Tuesday evening, I offered to drive the boys down there for an hour's practice. The guard came with us and sat under a horse chestnut as we bowled and batted, laughed and celebrated, staying out until the stars were quite visible overhead. We drove back in high spirits, happy that there'd now be two days of cricket in our week.

The next morning, I got a call from the captain of the local team. I'd deleted his number and it took me a moment to work out who it was. The groundsman had seen me in the nets with a bunch of Indian lads the night before, he said. I did the thing I do when I get angry, going first hot then very cold, and feeling my pulse in my throat. Before I could shape my response, he continued. The groundsman had said the lads were pretty decent. We were short a few on Sunday and did they fancy a game?

I don't want to make too much of what happened next. I suppose I could say that it was a lesson in what goes on when people are forced to see others as individuals rather than in abstract generalisations, or that it was a message about the innate goodness of your average Englishman, or the great solvent of cricket. It wasn't even the fact that Abdul-Ghani took all but two of our opponent's wickets and Hafez hit a beautiful, brutal half-century. It was, over tea after the game, the sight of the groundsman, who's in his early seventies, offering to introduce Abdul-Ghani to a man he knows at the county ground. It was the sense, I'm sure I only half-imagined, that this groundsman was already picturing himself shepherding Abdul-Ghani through the early years of his cricketing career, and then watching with pride as the wickets tumbled on a cloudless day at Lord's. If you boys need work, he said to them, he was sure he could find something. Minimum wage, mind, but it would be good to have you around. The butcher chipped in here that he was looking for someone to help him out at the weekend, while another said he needed a strong lad to help with the harvest. They asked the boys all the questions about life in Afghanistan that I'd been told not to ask and were given sad, eloquent answers.

At the end, as the team went off to the pub and I packed the boys into the car, the captain of the local side came and thanked me for driving them down. What a good bunch of lads, he said. Decent cricketers, too. Can you bring them back next week?

When I turned up on Wednesday, the boys had gone. No, I couldn't get in touch with them – data privacy, safeguarding. There had been a new intake of Eritreans and the Afghans had been moved into other accommodation. Would I mind taking the Syrian boys out for a game of football? I did, and carried on playing football with them every Wednesday until the centre closed that winter, all of the young people moved to a larger operation in a nearby town. I miss my games of cricket, though. I find myself wondering about those four boys, about whether they're still playing, and if they look back on those long, sunny afternoons as I do: as a gentle moment in a difficult year, a reminder that, for all of us, there is more that binds than divides.

Bridges

Aamer Hussein

Translated from the Urdu by Sabeeha Malek with the assistance of the author

1.

'Take me to the river,' I said to Nermin when we met at the Gare du Nord.

2.

I've always loved rivers, and the cities through which they pass. Cities are often too remote from rivers, or the river runs dry and leaves only a trickle of water that looks like a stream. I've seen a dried-up riverbed in Delhi, where washermen wash clothes in the yellow trickle, and people plant watermelons which they sell on the streets in summer. In Lahore, too, the river looks feeble and muddy. The grandest view is in Istanbul, but the lashing blue Bosphorus isn't a river, it's a strait, which divides the city in two like a river would.

I first met Nermin in Istanbul four years ago. She seemed quite settled there. She didn't agree with much of what her friends were saying about Erdogan.

'Let's wait and watch,' she'd say. 'I'm happy here because this city doesn't lay any claim on me. Perhaps your relationship with London's like that? I was neither born nor brought up here. When fighting broke out in Cyprus I was only nine or ten. Turkish was my language and I spoke it well but even today I use some words like a Cypriot would. But then I got married at twenty and moved to the States where I lived for many years with my husband.'

3.

Now, after four years, we were meeting in Paris. Since the last time I'd seen her Nermin had been wandering around the world. Europe. America, Australia. A month ago she'd written to me: *I've said farewell to Istanbul. I've given back the place to the landlady and come to Paris.*

She'd moved into her own little flat. On the phone, she'd said:

'I'm off to America in a few weeks and I'm going to be there for two months. Why don't you come and see me here?'

'Busy time. Marking student papers.'

'It's a bank holiday next Monday. Just come over for the day. You can take the train back in the evening.'

4.

I'd boarded the train in the morning, early. Two hours on the Eurostar and I was in Paris. The station was crowded and I didn't see her. In panic, I called her cell phone and there was no reply. I hadn't been in Paris for thirty-three years and I was a complete stranger there. I wondered what I'd do if I didn't find her.

Then someone called out my name. I turned to see Nermin running towards me in a red dress.

5.

'There are thirty-seven bridges in Paris,' she said as she led me to the river. 'Let's have lunch first, then I'll take you to the river.'

We stopped under the awning of Shakespeare and Company, the bookshop opposite the Gothic white fantasy of Notre Dame. We sat down on the open terrace of a restaurant nearby and talked. I felt as if I had done nothing more in all these years than travel, teach and write a few stories. A lot had happened to Nermin, though. Just a few days after the last time I'd seen her in Istanbul she'd left her husband and moved into her own flat. Her son was eighteen and engrossed in his studies. She couldn't take him with her but she didn't want to be too far from him. So she'd found a little room nearby. Now her son was twenty-three. He'd moved to Paris after completing his studies. Nermin had been travelling back and forth. After the events at Gezi Park she'd become disheartened with the divisions around her. She'd started to feel she wasn't any part of the city.

It isn't entirely dark, she'd written. *But the storm clouds are gathering.*

6.

Meanwhile she'd written some of her most beautiful stories, almost prose poems. Stories about brothers and sisters parting, about friendships breaking up over a child's broken toy, about passionate attachments born in the tumult of a political demonstration.

Brief, slight images, like the breath of a bird dying on the sleeve of the wind, like the castanets of a dancing gypsy, like a drop of blood from the paw of a wounded rabbit in the grass, like the last smouldering embers of the evening.

7.

We crossed the church gardens and came to a bridge.

'Stop here, I'll take a photograph,' she said.

The filigreed walls of the bridge were laden with bunches of artificial flowers in bright colours: red, yellow, blue, purple.

There were cloud reflections in the river's grey waters.

As I walked towards the wall I noticed that the flowers weren't flowers at all, they were locks: bunches of locks, big locks, small locks, heavy locks, little locks. Locks of all sizes, locks of all colours.

Nermin was laughing.

'Don't you know the story of this bridge?'

'No. Tell me.'

'You really don't know? This is the Pont des Arts, but now it's known as the Bridge of Lovers! Young lovers come here in the middle of the night, swear fidelity to each other, fasten a lock on the wall, lock it up and throw away the key into the Seine. No one can trace the origins of this custom. It's predicted that the weight of the locks will bring the walls down one day. Two American women recently filed a complaint about it. They even tried to break the locks with a hammer but the locks won't break. And all the keys are in the depths of the river.'

'Isn't there a young bride in one of your stories who comes to

Paris with her husband? Wandering around the streets of Paris they get into an argument. They reach a bridge and the husband threatens to jump into the river.'

'Yes, this is the bridge. I came here on my honeymoon. It was a snowy winter night but I didn't see any locks here then. And we didn't make any vows here or swear to stay together for ever. Well, all that... come on, let's move on, it's getting late.'

8.

A Metro journey in the afternoon's rush hour. Don't people have showers here? There are quite a few beggars in this opulent city, hanging around the station and the street corners. But then it occurs to me that we are all strangers in these cities of ours, and strangers we'll remain.

We got off the Metro. The afternoon was mild. We sat over an espresso in the shade of a tree. Two veiled African women passed by.

'No one takes me for a Muslim here.' Nermin sipped her coffee.

'So should all Muslims be wandering around wrapped in sheets?'

'But you're not an Arab, they say. Not all the world's Muslims are Arab, I retort. But you're so fair, and your hair is brown... what can I say to that, except for wishing I was brown too.'

'I'd gone to dinner at a friend's,' I said. 'An academic historian was trying to pick an argument about veiled women with the hostess, who writes about Mughal art. To begin with the lady tried to keep the conversation light, citing relative cultural values et cetera et cetera. Then I realised that the esteemed professor was trying to pull me into the argument. He addressed me directly and said: "In earlier days, migrants used to bring the seeds of their own progress with them which they planted in the new soil. Look at the Jews in America. Look at the children of immigrants. The sons of the illiterate became scientists and political theorists. But your Muslims have reversed the process! They come to the west with their antediluvian customs and want everyone to kowtow to them. They are squandering all our capital..." I had noticed that he'd been drinking quite a bit, and gave him a sharp response with references to the Second World War and then changed the subject. And I remembered how the election of Modi had driven a young friend of mine to consider abandoning his research in India to come back to London. Someone had told him that if he didn't like India, why didn't he go and blow himself up across the border? *Living here's becoming unbearable,* he'd written. *Even one's friends are becoming strangers.'*

I was waiting for Nermin's response to my unspoken question: *What brought you away from Istanbul, where you could call so many your own? Perhaps your memories of the island where you witnessed so many kinds of prejudice. Religion. Nation. Ethnic identity. And you couldn't escape these memories.*

But my wandering thoughts had taken me away from where we were. The day was on the wane. Soon I'd have to catch my train.

'Whenever I felt anxious in Istanbul I'd look out from my window at the Bosphorus.' Nermin's voice interrupted my reverie. 'But after the riots I didn't feel safe, walking around alone in the evenings. Here I spend evenings strolling on the riverbanks. From one bridge to another. I think as I wander. Faint outlines and broken phrases of new stories arise in my mind. But when I get home and sit down at my desk so many of those sounds and images have just slipped away. All the stories are lying around unfinished. Listen, aren't you seeing anyone these days?'

I was about to tell her. Instead I smiled and said: 'Where do I have the time for emotional entanglements?'

9.

So many stories remained untold during this short interlude. I just said, 'You'll be off to America now, then what's next?'

'This state of homelessness here – you could say that's where I feel most at home.'

She laughed. It was nearly time for me to leave for the station.

'Let's go home,' she said, 'we're not far. We can have a supper of bread and cheese before you take your train.'

10.

There were eleven minutes left before the train departed when I took my seat. Two hours to London, then another three quarters of an hour to reach home, it'll be midnight by the time I get in. I took out my notes for tomorrow's lecture from my bag. I had another long journey tomorrow.

Along with the pleasure of seeing Nermin I also felt a light sadness. Home, estrangement, faith, love – how we wander around in these tight concentric circles. Outside the sky was a fiery gold at 10 p.m. When will it be night? After seeing me off Nermin must be strolling from bridge to bridge in her red dress. Perhaps she'll walk from the lovers' bridge to the bridge of partings and then she'll reach her door. I closed my stinging eyes. 'Guess what I did when I got to Paris?' The gentle echo of Nermin's words was in my ears. 'I stood on the bridge and emptied my pockets of all the keys that I'd been carrying around in my pockets and purses for years and years. Keys for which I'd long ago lost the locks and I didn't even know where they came from. House keys. Keys to things left behind when I'd changed houses. Keys to wardrobes, chests of drawers, trunks. Keys of cars I'd driven long ago.'

But which of the thirty-seven bridges of Paris was she on? Not the bridge of lovers? I too have a key in my pocket and I have no idea to which door it belongs. Every time I look for something in my pocket my hand finds the same key. I'd like to throw it away in the river, I wanted to say, but Nermin wasn't there. And perhaps in my drowsiness I'd heard her say something she never said.

The train plunged into darkness as it entered the tunnel beneath the sea. On the other side was the border with England. I shut my eyes again.

In the Dark

Anjali Joseph

'The rain,' Ved said. 'I mean, obviously, people talk about it.' He looked out of the window. 'I just... I wasn't expecting quite this.'

Keteki's uncle smiled at him. 'Yes, yes, Ved,' he said. 'We have rain. And storms.' He got up from the table and wandered towards the bookshelves, taking with him one of the storm lanterns. The room otherwise was in darkness, except when lightning flashed, followed by an enormous clap of thunder. Massive volumes of water poured out of the sky.

Ved flinched. 'It sounds like the end of the world,' he said. 'Like the sky is cracking open.'

Jayanta turned to look at Ved, and the younger man thought he smirked. But he turned back to the bookshelf. 'I was looking for two things,' he said. 'A photograph album, you know, thought you might like to see some of Keteki's earlier days. Her mother, me, our family. And another thing, a book of proverbs and folk superstitions, quite interesting.'

'When did your sister pass away?' Ved asked.

There was a cough. 'Ved? I'm not quite sure I got your meaning.'

'Oh, sorry,' Ved said. 'I meant, when did she die. Sorry if you don't want to—'

The lamp in the hand of the older man bobbed its way back towards the table. Jayanta sat down. He sighed, and folded his arms. 'Ved,' he said. 'Forgive a terribly old-fashioned question, but what *are* your intentions towards my niece?'

Ved exhaled. 'Long term,' he said. 'I mean... long, long term. If she'll have me. I don't think – well, I don't really think I've been that clear about that with her. Everything happened quite fast, in a way. I mean, we met a year ago, but we've only been in the same place a few times – when I came here in the winter, and this summer in London.' He closed his eyes for a moment, remembering the joy, and deflation, of being with Keteki in this house last winter, before she disappeared.

Joy mama, as Keteki called him, nodded. 'I think I mentioned this, but she comes from quite a ruptured background. My sister is not an easy person, I'm afraid. Can be charming, incredibly so, when she wants to be.' He smiled. 'Her husband – my brother-in-law – came from a very good family. Money too. They were a brilliant couple when they first met. He was good looking, intelligent, just starting out in the tea trade. But he liked to drink.'

'They only had one child?'

Joy mama nodded. 'Though my sister lost a child before Ketu was born. But after her, her parents weren't in a position to have another. My brother-in-law was away a lot, my sister was in Guwahati, the child was sent between her aunt and me. But things went wrong, and we thought it would be better to send her to boarding school, in the north. Good school, but such a long way from here.' He wiped his eyes. 'There was nothing else to be done, but it was hard. She was only eleven or twelve years old. But her father was already in ill health – he died of cirrhosis you know, Ved, when Ketu was fifteen. Though she didn't see him much in the last few years. And then our troubles began in Assam. In the nineties it was a good thing for anyone who could to be away.'

Ved nodded.

'Mother and daughter are not close, Ved. My sister doesn't keep in touch. She moved to Dimapur quite some time back, and lives with a gentleman there.' There was a flash of lightning.

'She's not dead?' Ved said.

Joy mama laughed. 'Not even a little bit,' he said.

The thunder cracked hugely and wind made the trees thrash.

'This is a strange country,' Joy mama said.

'India?'

'Assam. So beautiful yet always being unmade. Earthquakes, floods, such fertile land. The river, of course. I wonder when the power will come back,' Joy mama said.

'To Assam?' said Ved.

'The electricity, Ved. If it doesn't return soon, the best thing is for us to eat and go to bed. Look at that.' A flying cockroach battered itself against the glass of the storm lamp. Joy mama tutted, and flicked it off, but not for long. 'We can go to the kitchen,' he said. 'The inverter only works for some rooms. So you haven't talked to Ketu? About your plans, or hopes?' he added, leading the way down the passage. Ved remembered bumping into Keteki here last year on their way to dinner.

Joy mama opened the door from the dining room into the kitchen, which was lit with a gentle glow.

'Is that a Lucifer?' Ved asked.

'Very likely,' said Joy mama. 'They give a pleasant light. It's running off the inverter anyway.'

Tuku sat at the table, reading the newspaper. Ved was slightly surprised to note how muscular were the younger man's shoulders. He wore a short-sleeved T-shirt over a long-sleeved one. There was a sense of ease in his posture.

'O, Dada,' Tuku said, and smiled at them.

Jayanta issued a series of coaxing instructions, patted Tuku on the shoulder, sighed, and said, 'Bade, I've told him we'll eat here. Do sit down.'

As they did, Joy mama added, 'One thing about you does remind me of Ketu. If you'll forgive me. A quality of not being at home. Did you go to boarding school?'

Ved shook his head. 'No,' he said. 'Lived at home in west London till I went to college. But, you know, maybe moving from India to England when I was eight. Maybe the kind of school I went to. It's true, there's no one place...' He thought of his flat, and felt a sense of respite, but not welcome. Although, in the weeks Keteki had often been there, even as he protected his independence, he'd begun to notice how nice it was to be at home with her.

'Would you like something to drink, Ved? A beer?'

'Sure,' said Ved.

Tuku brought a bottle, beaded with moisture. Joy mama poured two glasses, handed one to Ved, and clinked it. He shrugged himself back from the table to lean against the wall. 'Do you think she'll say yes?' he asked.

'To what?' Ved said. He realised how this sounded and added quickly, 'I mean – I haven't had a chance to think things through. I don't know what I should say, or ask.'

'Yes, well, I suppose,' said Joy mama, frowning into his beer, 'that would be a good idea.'

Ved hesitated. 'I know I want to do this properly,' he said. 'Can I ask you something?'

'Ask away, Ved.'

'In your life,' Ved said, 'have you felt – that you knew what to do? For the future? And later, felt you decided correctly?'

The older man laughed, then extended a large paw. 'Sorry, sorry Ved,' he said. 'I'm afraid wisdom hasn't yet descended. I'm not sure it will. I do know I resisted certain things, including having a family, because I couldn't tell what the future would bring. How I might feel. And yet,' he smiled, and looked down at the palm of his hand, 'for the most part I've lived a very quiet life, in my family home, surrounded by those we know. There are elements of my existence no one knows. But that's true of everyone.' He looked Ved in the eye.

Ved felt behind his collar. After a pause, he wondered, 'Does anyone really decide what to do? Or are periods of lethargy just followed by spasms of action?'

The older man laughed. 'That's well put, Ved. I don't know. In my case, though, there have been long periods of contentment. The more I sat still, you know, the less I felt like moving outside that space. I'm not advocating it as a life.'

Ved leaned on his elbows, and drank his beer. He watched Tuku move, loose limbed yet compact, and envied his grace. He was always looking at others and finding their way of being effortless. He went on drinking his beer and imagining different futures with Keteki. In one, wearing slightly seventies clothing, they smilingly looked after two young children. He realised he'd conflated memories of childhood with his crush on Katharine Ross in *The Graduate*. In another image, he and Keteki fought constantly, and sometimes had incandescent sex. In a third, he was at an airport lounge, waiting desolately for her. Even if he got what he wanted, there were so many ways to fuck up.

'I worry,' he said. 'I worry about making mistakes.'

'In one view,' said Joy mama, 'there is no such thing as a mistake. Of course, that's quite an abstracted view. Sort of, What does it matter anyway?' He chuckled.

'My work,' Ved said. 'The Lucifers. It's very mysterious. It was all going so well. But now these defects. The lightbulb was properly tested. I saw the reports. I don't understand… Something is happening.'

'I suppose these things aren't uncommon,' Joy mama said. 'There was that new car a few years ago. The Nano? Some of them burst into flames or something when they were brand new.'

Ved nodded. 'But it seems as though someone doesn't want the Lucifer to succeed,' he said. 'There was that fire, earlier, in the factory.'

'Well, people have their reasons to be disgruntled,' Joy mama said. There was an almighty crack of thunder, a howl of wind, and the lights went out. Tuku said something.

'The inverter's blown,' said Joy mama.

'Oh,' said Ved.

'We have candles, of course,' Joy mama said. He said something to Tuku, who acquiesced and went away. Ved looked at the moving shadows that seemed to come from the door into the dining room. He had a sense of the house behind its daytime appearance. In the dark, physical objects were inquisitive presences. The life of the family, too, appeared more mobile and quick. He had an image of his mother, sitting in a living room in Hounslow, not in their house, upright on a golden velour sofa, talking to someone Ved didn't remember about Ved and his brother. 'He swears like a trooper,' she said of Ved, not without pride. But this was the daylight image. The night-time one was different: thumps from his parents' bedroom, the sound of his mother's voice like a raw edge of broken glass, quietly and insistently berating Ved's father, Ved clutching the edge of a cheap duvet and, later, wanking into tissues while he thought about the thighs and arses of whichever girls he'd stared at that day.

There was light again, a little: Tuku came back, with the storm lanterns. Outside, there were cracks and creaks of breaking wood. 'The trees,' said Joy mama sadly. But he too was a different creature in the penumbra: more fluid, less forthcoming.

'Keteki,' said Ved.

Her uncle, quizzical, refined, smiled at him.

'She never talks about her parents,' Ved said.

The older man inhaled. 'If you'd seen Ketu as a child,' he said. 'She was very loving, very curious. Little round-faced thing, very sweet. But by the time she was ten or eleven things were going wrong. My sister,' he sighed, 'is very spoiled. She was the baby of the family. But my brother-in-law fell in love with her immediately. It's just that it's exhausting, in the end, to try to please someone who refuses to be happy. He was a very charming person, and before too long, that charm wasn't reserved for my sister.'

'Ah,' said Ved.

'We are old-fashioned here, Ved,' said Joy mama.

'In India?' said Ved.

'In Assam.'

'Right.'

'The family is more important than an ideal of romantic love, I suppose,' Joy mama said.

Tuku came to ask if they would eat. Joy mama said yes. The young man brought to the table a pork curry, rice and a dish of greens.

'Mustard leaves, Ved,' Joy mama said. 'You'll like them.' Tuku sat with them, and ate neatly with his right hand. Ved and Joy mama used forks. As the meal ended, the light clicked back on.

'Oh good, good, that's very good,' said Joy mama. It was still raining, but calmly, like rain in another place. A couple of enormous cockroaches ran around on the floor. Tuku went to hit them on the head and throw them out of the door. The storm lamps were still lit. The kitchen was messy – Tuku hadn't been able to see what he was doing as he worked.

'It's good of you to come to see us, Ved, especially when Ketu is in London,' Joy mama said. He, Ved and Tuku sat on the little sofa in the front room. The television was on. 'Where are you off to tomorrow?'

Ved sighed. 'I have to go to Bombay. I'll fly out from there. But I need to meet Mr Ganesh and decide what to do next. I wanted—'

He stopped, because in the break from the Assamese news, a familiar ad played. A little boy was trying to study at a table in a harshly lit room. In the next room, a husband and wife were quarrelling. Suddenly Mahendra Singh Dhoni, the cricketer, appeared. 'Need more light in your life?' he asked, dubbed into Assamese. The next moment, the voiceover said, 'Everlasting Lucifer' and the little boy at the table was studying happily under a golden glow. The couple in the other room smiled at each other; the husband stroked the wife's hair. It was almost the same picture, but everything was different. 'Ebherlasting Lucifer,' said the voiceover. 'Lasting happiness.'

'Lovely advertisement,' Joy mama said.

'Thanks,' Ved said. 'I don't know if we should have waited though, with all these production issues. Um, can I talk to you?'

Joy mama was slumped like an out-of-shape wrestler. 'Talk? Ah, yes Ved. Do talk.' He looked at Ved and sighed. 'You want to go in another room?'

'Yes please,' Ved said.

Joy mama rose, said something to Tuku who smiled at him, then beckoned Ved. 'We'll go to my room. I don't think you've seen it,' he said.

It was small and bare, with two chairs, a table, a bed and a framed photo of a man in orange with a halo.

'Sit down, Ved,' Joy mama said. He indicated an armchair near the bed and scooped off a sweater and one of the cats from it. The cat gave Ved an indignant look and flounced onto the bed. Joy mama sat on a chair facing Ved.

'Um,' Ved said. 'I've been thinking about it, and I want to ask Keteki to marry me.'

Her uncle regarded him. 'You've been thinking about it since dinner?'

'I want to make a life with her,' Ved said.

'But you don't really know each other, do you?' Joy mama folded his arms. 'Forgive me. I want my niece to be happy.'

'You don't think I'm the man for her?'

The older man laughed. 'Is there a man for the job? Is it man's work? I'd be glad to see her with someone and happy, I know that. But I don't *know*, Ved, if she's like her mother or even like me. I don't know if everyone is meant to live with others.'

'Can you tell me more about it?' Ved asked.

'Wouldn't it be better to ask her?'

'There are some things she doesn't talk about,' Ved said.

'Perhaps,' said her uncle, 'she doesn't wish to.'

Ved nodded. 'Do – do you think there's anyone else?' he asked, and fixed his eyes on Joy mama.

'I've no idea, Ved. Not that I know of. I mean, countless people no doubt, but I'm not aware of a serious attachment. Look, I'm not going to break any confidences. But I will try to help you. I don't *know* if things can work between you. I don't know, quite frankly, if you have what it takes.' He peered at Ved, removed his glasses, sighed, and rubbed his eyes.

'What might it take?' said Ved.

Joy mama sighed. 'Patience,' he said.

'I can be patient.'

'Can you? The point about patience is that you have to have it just when you can't take things any more.' Joy mama chuckled. 'It's taken me years to learn this. I don't want to be a sententious old bore but – oh, perhaps I do. I've put up with enough of them, God knows. In any case, you've got to let people be as they are. That's it.' He opened out his hands, palms up. 'That's the secret. Let people be, and in this case, love them – love her – as she is.'

'How is she, would you say?'

Joy mama looked at his fingers, which he'd splayed out. He smiled to himself, the secretive line near his eye appearing. 'I wouldn't like to try to *fix* her, like a butterfly with a pin through it,' he said. 'But there is something very joyful in her.'

'Yes,' said Ved quickly.

The older man smiled at him. 'But also a sadness that's a little too much in a young person,' he said. 'She is very aware of human frailty. How could she not be, with an upbringing like that? I sometimes feel if Ketu had a real home of her own she would be able to do anything.'

'I'd like to give her that,' Ved said. As he spoke he felt a warmth in his chest, but his mind queried: Stability? You? And it was true that he and Keteki barely knew each other, in a way. Ved had this evening acquired a potential mother-in-law. Details, he decided.

'You'd need to be steady for her, Ved,' Joy mama said. 'People who – people who have lived through difficult times are not always comfortable to be around. I don't – but really, I should stop talking.'

He raised his eyebrows and stood. 'It's late, Ved. I should sleep. Do you have everything you need?'

'Yes,' Ved said. He got up too. 'Thank you so much. You've been so kind. I really—'

'Goodnight, Ved,' said Joy mama. He raised his hand in farewell as he went into the bathroom. A light went on.

Tuesday Lunch

Leila Aboulela

Nadia is eight and she can read now. She can read the lunch menu for today, Tuesday, stuck on the door of the gym. The gym is used as a dining room during lunch. Tables with benches fastened to them cover the white lines on the floor where the children bounce balls and slide beanbags. Now, as the children chatter and crowd in the queue, as the delicious smells waft through from the kitchen amidst the clutter of spoons and trays, Nadia finds it hard to believe that this is the gym room. If she were to take her skirt off right now, stand in her white shorts, run or jump, how wrong that would be, how out of place. Yet in the afternoon this is what she will be doing and there will be no smells of food, no plates, no tables, and if you start to eat something right in the middle of gym, how naughty you would be. These thoughts give her a feeling of pride, she is older now, she understands the difference, she can behave in a correct way and as a blessing, as a reward, blend with everyone else, not stand apart. For this was bad behaviour, this was naughtiness, being pointed out, the centre of attention, the general disapproval for being different. You play quietly, you are alone in your own world with imaginary friends.

And then if you do something wrong, even if you don't mean to, the peace is shattered, Lateefa snaps in irritation, the child's voice rises, 'Mrs Benson, Nadia broke my pencil.'

Yet knowing that she can leave the queue, that she can let go of her tray and run pretending it is time for gym, that nothing is physically restraining her, fills her with a thrill. A fear that somehow the control will slip, that she will slide to a younger, innocent age, only that now forgiveness will not come so easily as it did years before. 'You knew you were doing something wrong,' Lateefa would say, pinching her arm, 'it's not that you didn't know, you knew, so WHY did you do it?' Nadia is now eight and she knows that wilful disobedience is not something that adults forgive easily.

The menu is written in black in Mrs Hickson's handwriting. She hangs it up on Monday and it shows the lunches for the whole week. Sometimes, before Nadia goes to sleep at night, she lies awake and tries to remember the menu for the rest of the week, listing the items one by one. Monday night is the most challenging, Thursday night the easiest. Today, Tuesday, is Chicken Risotto, Pork Pie, Mashed Turnips, Boiled Potatoes, Tomato and Nut Salad, Black Forest Gateau and Fruit Yoghurt. Nadia knows it must be the Chicken Risotto for her and then she has a choice of the vegetables and dessert.

Nadia likes chicken. At home Lateefa buys *halal* chicken, travelling by bus every week to the Pakistani butcher on Finchley Road, and carrying four of them home in one of the green Marks & Spencer bags that she collects. Chicken Risotto, the potatoes (not the turnips, definitely not the turnips) and the cake, this is what she will take. And Mrs Hickson knows about the pork, so when it is

Nadia's turn, Mrs Hickson will give her the chicken with what Nadia calls her giant tweezers. Mrs Hickson knows about the pork because Lateefa told her. Lateefa told everyone: the headmaster, who was very polite; Mrs Benson, Nadia's teacher, who said that Nadia can very well read the menu and there is always a choice (a reply Lateefa found unconvincing); and finally Mrs Hickson herself, who showed great interest and concern.

However, Lateefa argued later to Hamdy, if I saw one of these poor children whose crazy parents are vegetarians eating meat, I wouldn't stop him, would I? 'You would if it was your job to do so,' he said and promptly fell asleep. But just to make sure, she decided to bribe them, the headmaster, the teacher and especially Mrs Hickson. They of course never imagined they were being bribed. The headmaster got an Egyptian alabaster ashtray and an ivory letter opener. His teenage daughter, horrified at the thought that an African elephant was slain for its tusks, threw it in the attic, where it languished among jigsaw puzzles with missing pieces and headless dolls. The ashtray accidentally found its way to the school jumble sale (none of the family smoked), where Lateefa winced when she saw it and paid thirty pence to take it back home.

Mrs Benson was happier with her present, a pair of earrings with a pharaonic design, while Mrs Hickson was thrilled with her cotton cushion covers. She bought a filling for them and scattered them on her double bed. She thought they gave the room a somewhat mysterious, 'ethnic' look. 'I would love to go to Cairo one day,' she told Lateefa, 'my father was there during the war.' Lateefa told her the joke about the Egyptian village where suddenly all the babies born had blonde hair and blue eyes. There was apparently a British garrison stationed nearby during the war. But Mrs Hickson did not laugh.

It is not Mrs Hickson serving out the hot meal this Tuesday and Nadia suddenly finds herself facing a young woman she has never seen before, a woman who is asking 'Pork pie or chicken?' And to Nadia it is as if the whole room has changed or that she, Nadia, has changed. If she answers 'pork pie' or even just the 'pie', no need to say the forbidden word, just say 'pie', this new dinner lady will not be surprised, she will pick one up with the giant tweezers and put it on Nadia's plate. It will sit with the potatoes and the salad. But where is Mrs Hickson? She might suddenly appear. 'No pork for Nadia,' she will say, looking behind her shoulders, and the new dinner lady will turn with a sigh, a slight irritation, 'Well, why didn't you say so child?' and give Nadia the chicken.

Then Nadia asks about Mrs Hickson. The children behind her are impatient, the lady's hand is poised in the air holding the tweezers. But Nadia must ask, she swallows and speaks. 'Off ill,' the reply. Mrs Hickson has never been ill, not before, and Nadia feels there must be a pause, a time to ponder, a time to take in the newness.

(Mrs Hickson is at home nursing a bladder infection, clutching a hot water bottle to her stomach, drinking water to flush the germs out of her system. She glances at the clock, twelve noon, and does not think of Nadia, or that she would be now standing dishing out the meals. She only thinks *dammit, three more hours until I take the second tablet, when will these antibiotics start to work?*)

'If you don't want a hot meal, you can have cheese and biscuits with the potatoes,' the lady says, already looking at the boy behind Nadia in the queue.

'Pie,' whispers Nadia, 'I'll have the pie.'

It tastes like chicken. It doesn't taste bitter or sour. Not like the other things Lateefa forbids her to taste like perfume and orange peel. It tastes like ordinary food. Nadia pushes ketchup on it with her knife and it tastes better with the ketchup. The other children talk while they are eating, a normal day, a normal lunch hour. Yesterday Nadia was like them, but today the lunch break seems infinite, real, glittering. Tracy, Nadia's best friend, is eating the chicken risotto. Tracy, who on other days ate pork pie while Nadia watched and wondered. Tracy, who brings bacon-flavoured crips to school and Nadia doesn't try them. Today, of all days, Tracy is eating the chicken risotto. And Nadia feels a sudden dislike for her friend.

In the classroom, after lunch, it is time for mathematics. Tracy is not good in maths, not like Nadia, and while Nadia divides Tracy is still multiplying. Nadia's workbook is neat, she works quickly, moving her lips as if she is talking to herself. When she finishes a page Mrs Benson checks it and stamps a picture of a boy rushing past on a skateboard. 'Keep it up', the slogan above his head says. Sixteen divided by four, twelve divided by three, fifteen divided by five. Easy. And Nadia worries a little about what she would do if the sixteen were divided by five, if the picture in the workbook showed three children with ten sweets to share among them. It wouldn't work then, they wouldn't be able to share. Nadia pushes a feeling away, a tired feeling, it is such a long time since lunch, since breakfast. But she can't think about that and can't even think of the chocolate bar she and Lateefa will share when she gets home from school.

There is a bad feeling in her chest and in her throat and she wants it to go away. Ten divided by two, six divided by three, eighteen divided by six. She is stuck, eighteen divided by six… if it was divided by nine that would have been easy but six, eighteen divided by six. Maybe it is one of those numbers that couldn't be divided, like the three children couldn't share ten sweets. The numbers seem jumbled now on the page, time seems so slow. Nadia thinks she should get up, walk up to Mrs Benson bending over Tracy's red hair. When she looks my way I will speak to her, thinks Nadia and she puts her head on the workbook. It feels cool to her forehead, her forehead is damp, the black numbers on the page loom close to her, the boy on the skateboard grins maliciously and she closes her hurting eyes.

'Nadia, Nadia.' Mrs Benson's voice filters through and Nadia lifts her face up, swallows but it is too late. A gush, the sound of a tap opening, a flood on the workbook, on Nadia's lap, on Mark's pencils, a speck of potato on Brian's left arm. And on the soaked boy with the skateboard, a pink remnant of pork pie, his face still grinning through, 'Keep it up.' And Nadia keeps it up when Mrs Benson with remarkable agility positions the waste-paper basket strategically in front of her. Impossible to stop, even when Brian says 'Ukk, Ukk, Ukk,' and continues to say it, even with Tracy spluttering with laughter, covering her mouth with her hands, her knees clenched together, and even while Mark whines gently, 'Mrs Benson, I need a new pencil.'

There is no relief. Intervals but no relief. In one of those intervals Nadia is led to the toilet. Mrs Benson is kind, helping her clean her jumper, telling her to wash her face, not angry, not shouting. Nadia is afraid she will be angry; the mess in the class – who is going to clean it? And the workbook – what will happen to the workbook?

In the toilet the rest of her lunch floods out, easier now, not so thick and clogged, smoother. The red of ketchup, orange juice, lots of orange juice. And at home, when Lateefa finally picks her up and they go home, there is nothing left. She retches, her stomach squeezes itself but there is nothing left, just a dull, still pain in her muscles. A drained feeling, her body trembling.

'Get into bed, Nadia, sleep and you'll feel better, I won't let you eat anything else today. Tomorrow *Insha Allah* you'll be better.' In her pyjamas Nadia feels clean, her room smells nice, the sheets are cool and comforting.

'What is it that you ate that made you so sick? What did you have for lunch?'

'Chicken,' says Nadia, her nose in the pillow, her eyes closed, and then, after a while, 'Mrs Hickson was off ill today.'

'What else did you eat?'

'Black Forest Gateau.'

'What's that?'

'A cake, Mama, a chocolate cake.'

'It must have been the cream then. Old cream, bad for your

stomach. Go to sleep now, I'm going downstairs.' Relief, an empty stomach, at last relief and sleep will come easy now.

Nadia opens the cloakroom cupboard but it is not a cloakroom any more. It is her aunt Salwa's flat in Cairo. It doesn't look exactly like Tante Salwa's flat. It is more untidy, darker, narrow like the cloakroom. Her cousin Khalid is sitting on a chair, looking out of the window. Nadia climbs into his lap and he puts his arms around her, and his cheek rubs against her chin. She asks him what he is looking at without speaking, and he shows her the busy street below, the man blowing his horn selling candy floss, another with a large rack balanced in front of his bicycle filled with pitta bread. And Mrs Hickson standing alone in front of a table covered with pork pies, a table like the ones that Nadia eats lunch on at school. The giant tweezers in her hands, a placard with the picture of the boy on the skateboard showing the price, eighteen divided by six pence. Three, says Nadia to Khalid, three pence, but it is as if Khalid can't hear her. No one is going to buy these pies, he says.

Nadia is awake and hungry. The house is silent and dark. She has missed children's BBC, missed Hamdy's key turning in the lock on the front door. She has missed dinner. Lateefa will have told Hamdy about her being ill and sudden tears come to Nadia's eyes imagining how anxious and sad he must have been. He will have opened the door and looked at her while she slept, the way parents do on TV.

Tomorrow at school they will call her Nauseous Nadia, they will write Nozeus Nadia, NN for short. She will be hurt and ashamed. She will hope that they will forget the whole thing like magic, as if it didn't take place. But now she is hungry.

She wanders to her parents' bedroom. She can hear Hamdy snoring. Lateefa wakes up as if she was not asleep, clear and lucid and bright as if she was waiting for Nadia. She holds her daughter's cheek against her own to check her temperature. Nadia puts her arms around her and Lateefa says she will make toast and that Nadia should go back to bed.

Nadia can smell the toast, the smell made more delicious by the stillness of the night, the hunger she feels. Lateefa brings the toast with jam and they both sit up on Nadia's bed, covering themselves with the pink and orange quilt. The toast has strawberry jam on it and it is sweet and warm. Lateefa feels soft and Nadia leans against her arms, she can smell the jam and the bread. She wonders why her mother looks so beautiful now in her sleeveless cotton nightdress, not like when she picks Nadia up from school.

They giggle, it doesn't matter about the crumbs falling on the bed. They drink tea without any milk. No milk for a bad stomach, Lateefa says. The mug of tea is too hot for Nadia to hold and Lateefa must hold it for her in between sips. Lateefa has been teaching her a short chapter from the Qur'an, *Surat El-Ekhlas*, for some days now and Nadia can say it all by herself. 'In the Name of Allah, the Compassionate, the Merciful. Say: He is Allah, the One and Only. Allah, the Eternal, the Absolute. He begetteth not, nor is He begotten and there is none comparable unto Him.'

Lateefa kisses Nadia. 'Clever girl, not one mistake. When we go to Cairo you can show Khalid and Tante Salwa and they will be so proud of you.'

Now Lateefa takes the empty mugs away and it is time for Nadia to sleep. As sleep approaches, Nadia thinks that her mother must have cast a spell on all the wrong things Nadia should not do. Bewitched pork pies, so that even when she wanted them, they, of their own accord, rejected her.

Emily Brontë's Bath

Tiffany Murray

A granite lintel, strong as sisterly love
protects it on this blasted hill.
It's lasted centuries,
your bath.

Was it you who lugged it here
up your father's field,
behind your father's parsonage?
Was it you: tall, wiry as a lamping lurcher,

with your cook-steady hands, who shoved it
through this drystone wall – cursing probably –
until each enamel end poked out into each field
for buck-toothed sheep to suck on?

Or did you lasso a chain tight around
Keeper's neck, yelling, 'Do it, lad!'
as the poor dog – used to your tormenting –
dragged the bath up through the heather?

At last, you thought, no more shared water with adoring
sisters. No more lathered confessions, carbolic ambitions.
No more chairs backed into the bathroom door in case a
brother, drunk from the Black Lion, takes a wrong turn.

No more of that;
for up here it's you and the tub, Emily.
You wait days for Pennine rain to fill it
and you slip in, deliciously alone.

The bath of the poem still sits on the hill behind Haworth parsonage.

Emily Brontë preferred a certain 'other-ness' even before the myth-making: she often turned her face to the wall at supper, wouldn't speak when spoken to, wouldn't answer the parsonage door, wasn't keen on leaving the kitchen or Tabby, and when bitten by a possibly rabid dog she took a hot poker from the fire and cauterized the wound (we've read Shirley, *right?). She was also an excellent shot and a brilliant pianist. A singular woman many of us would like to meet, although I doubt she would have enjoyed our company.*

Point for Lost Children

A. L. Kennedy

Old ladies get away with things.

She's getting away with a lot, but I don't mind. I'm just making that observation, because she is here and sitting with me and we're chatting, kind of chatting, and nothing about us is causing any bother. There was bother before, but now an old lady's involved the whole of this situation has been turned. I could even lean back at this juncture, shut my eyes and imagine we're relaxed and in a café, one that we've chosen as our latest favourite place. Or maybe we're side by side and feet up in her living room, or resting for a moment while we attend an informal display that's to do with community art.

We're sitting together on the floor, but people do that sometimes, it's not unusual. There is nothing unusual about us and maybe we're not friends, but also we might be. So many things could be possible. I might be a newcomer, fresh in her street, and she's popped round like a friendly person to make offers and find things out. That's one of the things old ladies get away with – the curiosity. Nobody can resist when they make enquiries.

She walked right up to me with intention, as if we'd arranged to meet and finally catching sight of my face was making her day run according to plan. She leaned in and smiled, paused – like she was waiting for the next right beat in her personal music – and then she sat. Her hip bumped against me, soft and friendly, while she wriggled her way down. She's slow but very flexible. As she settled, she said, 'Budge up.'

I budged.

She asked, 'So how was this morning?'

There are questions you stop being used to. Your talking clots under your tongue and you miss it for a while and then you don't and starting the whole procedure again begins to scare you. I've limited myself to *thank you* for quite a while. That doesn't always go well, maybe because my timing isn't right. My personal music has no beat.

I'm wrong a lot.

She's all rhythm and she's got information about the weather and parliament and the best place to buy fruit. Her voice tumbles down and then flicks up. I think there's a bird which does that in its flight. Her eyes are very dark like a bird's eyes.

Birds' eyes are dark, I think, except for eagles and those more complicated kinds of things that kill other birds and creatures.

Everything indicates that she is a little bit crazy, but in a kind way. Craziness is an accelerant for personalities: you pour it over kindness and the kindness flares up and gets kinder. It works the same way on the opposite stuff as well.

But the opposite stuff is not to be dwelled on, so I count the steps that lead up to the street, count when feet come down them and when they climb. That keeps my head from being invaded.

I don't count out loud and I do also listen to her while she tells me her morning hasn't been bad. Her back is grumpy – she says *grumpy* with a smile as if she forgives it, or at least sympathises. She reports that she is liking the start of the sunshine and that it is cheerful, or cheering, or some word in that area.

I suppose I agree that it is cheerful or cheering or some word in that area.

And people pass us and I know without checking that they're not thinking *junkie, junkie, junkie, junkie, drunk.* Their faces are not at present expressing that.

We aren't precisely cheerful right now, though. We're shifted out beyond the cheer and my fingers are getting cold, somehow, or my arms.

Because this is a sign that circumstances want to close in and invade me, I try to find something to count about her clothes, her things.

She has a pair of those extendable walking poles, like she's exploring a mountain, only of course not and neither of us thinks she is. There would have been times when I'd have swerved her, avoided, in case of her being a risk, but at this not precisely cheerful exact period in my life I have limited options.

I can't count a pair – it's useless for counting.

But I do like her.

Big daft orangey skirt, she's wearing, with a big daft orangey shirt flopped over it and on top of that is a long red waistcoat. So many layers would make her a bundle if she was plump, but with her they just soften the outline of this tiny, wiry form. She isn't quite aiming for Buddhist Monk, but could very well pass for A Buddhist Monk's Proud Mum. If there was a uniform for that.

She could very well pass.

She could very well pass for forty-three in the dusk with a light behind her.

That's from Trial by Jury *which is by Gilbert and Sullivan.*

I know that.

Bouncy white trainers. Pair of trainers. And a scarlet pageboy cut – is what that style is called. Her hair must be naturally white because the dye job is raging out, uninterrupted, and what with her being so short and softened in her outlines it makes her look like she's a toy.

A gonk – that's what she is. When I was a girl I had loads of them. I lined them up along my windowsill. The light faded their colours, but I didn't mind, because they were friendly in spite of it, they were steadfast. I had more than anyone.

She's talking about my generation and it being such a sin what's happening. She's nodding her red, red head.

I had a lovely childhood.

Over her shoulder, there's a cloth bag that seems Tibetan, I think Tibetan. In a film she would be secretly a warrior with kung fu skills. She'd have dignified pensioner moves, but you'd still end up flat on your back and out cold if you were a bastard and defied her. Only a bastard would oppose her and her venerable power.

Or she'd be a retired social worker in a play that West End people watch.

It's better to keep the head racing.

I make a guess and a guess and a guess and a guess and then count the guesses. I'd rather count buttons, but there are none.

Her name ought to be Sky, or River, Isthmus, Archipelago – something geographical.

I have Higher Geography.

She isn't called Isthmus, she's called Marilyn.

I did O Grades and then Highers – they were the qualifications in Scotland at the time. I got Higher History, Maths, English, Biology and Geography. I don't have my certificates, but there must be records. You can take Advanced Highers now, but we had Sixth Year Studies. You had to write a dissertation, which was meant to be good practice for uni.

It wasn't practice for anything. They were a pish certificate. Folk laughed at them and there you'd been, trying your best to get them and you needn't have bothered and more fool you.

You always try your best, but you never get any practice at what matters. That's why you get invaded.

You follow the rules and are a good and a hard-working girl who always tries her best, but you make no difference. You're not designed to.

In the end people hate you. They don't know who you are and they hate you anyway, which isn't what you were told was going to happen.

Marilyn's face lets you know that she is mature, but being embracive about it.

Embracive.

I should be able to say what I want in my choice of expressions.

I should have that.

It should count when I haven't been wrong. It should be kept for the record.

Marilyn is embracing her condition and liking the things she is and there's no proper reason why she shouldn't and that's her choice.

We had a button tin at home: tortoiseshell and glass and pearl and toggles and fancy ones and the leather kind for cardigans.

I was going to make one of my own. A home isn't only furniture and somewhere to have a bath, or pillowcases in a stack that smell of your clean, warm wash and being looked after. You have to create your spaces for silliness, too. And that's for you and for who you love and for if you have kids and otherwise, why be an adult?

There's a shine on her, as if she's enjoying everything at least a little bit for the whole of the time she's awake and maybe while she's sleeping too. Marilyn seems like a person with sleep to spare.

She tells me her daughter was called Abby, which I'm guessing was short for Abigail, but I could be wrong.

Little girl with her fingers all aswim in buttons and the rushing noise of them.

I'm wrong a lot.

Although I'm listening while she says stuff it seems that I can't speak. This is a foolish shame and wasted opportunity.

I'm wrong a lot.

When she headed for me, she met my eyes and her face said I was going to be today's next thing to enjoy. Her smile was in anticipation of personal interactions. So I should be enjoying this and anything else would be a sin and because I don't work any more.

It's on my papers that I am challenged by personal interactions.

The people who hate me ignore my papers.

I've lost count of my guesses.

But we are a pair – *one, two* – and we are sitting on the floor together in Leicester Square Underground Station and we are getting away with it. I salute us and the awesome power of old ladies.

Just I don't mention it out loud.

I'm wrong a lot.

But we're not in the way.

When she saw me I must have been like a good shell on her beach, a collectible one that you dust off and take home in your pocket. She has collected me.

And oldness gets lonely, I would imagine. People die on you, so you go and seek others out.

It's only the good people who die. The shits and bastards, they last for ever. They have drunk everyone's strengths.

I bet that Marilyn cultivates young chums, the type to outlast her. She probably takes an interest in women who haven't quite flowered yet and need coaxing. I can easily picture her being keen about canoeing, or going off hiking up hills with her poles, just wandering everywhere across unstable countries where she'll be safe because she'll be honestly nice to everyone and the locals will take to her and act with gentle vigilance on her behalf.

She thinks the world smiles a lot. That's because of who she is, not because of the world.

I'd reckon that some of her young chums might even think she was a bit too full-on for them, too much. She's the unstoppable sort. Her neck's nothing but stretch and tendons, as if she's decided she has to be stripped down for action at this stage. She'll head up to summits with the boots and the poles working away and her chums will be soft and breathless from hanging about at unis or going to clubs, or eating junk because their kids are young and leave them tired and that's when you want to eat rubbish.

My mum didn't eat rubbish and neither did I. She wouldn't let me.

I started out in the prime of health.

I got good Highers.

I went to uni.

Sarah has application and will make us proud.

I was bang on the money all the time – when she stops talking I'll try and tell her that.

I only went to clubs for the dancing. I couldn't get enough of it. I wasn't much to look at, but guys would take an interest when they saw me move. I'd turn them away, though. I knew that not one of them would be able to keep up. I had good taste and determination.

I'll tell her that, too. Marilyn's probably a bit of a dancer.

She's got a tan: the hazelnuts and old leather type. I'd say she does the outdoors swimming, or something like that. You get that boiled sort of brown with being outside in the whole of the weather, not just the sun. I see it a lot. And I see where her hand is touching mine and we could be the same person, shade for shade. We could be this one woman holding her own hand and lacing fingers between fingers, because it's comfort.

I'm wrong a lot.

Marilyn feels as if she has a high thread count: silky. That's age, though. You end up smooth because each of your moments has rubbed against you and the friction wasn't hard enough to notice at the time, but now here's the evidence. You get worn, everybody does.

She's telling me things about Abby, about her daughter. It's sort of hard to listen, but there was this daughter and she got in some way ill. I can taste the suicide coming. Even without the word being said yet, it's clear.

Our hands are wet because Marilyn's crying on them. She's a very wet crier.

In my assessment I had to tell them about the suicidal thoughts, because their process is that they need to look right the way inside you, taste all the dirty places and invade and make you think they understand you, before they say that you're a liar. They take everything shameful to make you shamed. I had to tell them in which direction I've got to wipe my arse and why I can't reach or twist the way a normal person should and how doing everything, doing all the things, doing my life has got so difficult after what happened.

And then they lied about me.

They're the liars.

And her hands are soaking and my hands are soaking and it's like we are washing something, cleaning something.

And they're the ones that lie and they take their shame and they load it onto other people.

Being able to dress yourself and come to an interview, that isn't the same as working at a job, as every day managing to go and do a job.

And their lies are so lovely: that I don't hurt and don't need medication, that I can walk to the shops and carry home groceries, that nothing scares me, that I have a normal range of movement, that I am almost fit and well and will get better and be happy and work will make me free.

I can't explain how much I want them to be right.

I can't explain how much.

Marilyn has stopped talking. I've lost when this happened. It can't have been more than a minute ago. I don't want to be rude and this is when she probably wants me to say things back to her. I squeeze her hand instead, because you do that when you're sympathetic about someone's pain, but have mislaid your ways to say so.

I wrote essays. I was full up with dates and remembering and measurements and thoughts.

Fastidious.

I can't fill in the papers all in one day now. It takes a long time. I'm as stupid as Bobby kept saying.

I get things wrong a lot.

The end of the daughter's story will definitely be that she kills herself – that's why she's stopped telling it. All the stories end with killing yourself. The daughter took herself out of this shit and turned off her head and made it numb and didn't need to count any more or do whatever else she needed to keep on and on and on.

I hear that I've started speaking, the mouth working again. I'm saying, 'I'm sorry. I'm so sorry. Sorry.'

I don't say, *We were being cheerful. We were talking about which programmes we like on Radio 4 and it was all normal and cosy and when someone came, a Tube person in the Tube uniform – which is a pretty good uniform, I like it unless it's shouting – when the man came you said you were feeling poorly and that I was looking after you and not to worry. You said your problem was to do with the heat and we'd be OK really soon. And that was the opposite of suiciding and that's what I need and you're meant to be kind. You are a kind person. If you're going to talk about killing herself, killing myself, if you're going to flatten down the ramparts I put up against it, then you have to make me safe again afterwards. At least you could give me something I can count.*

'So sorry.'

Marilyn nods and then her hand starts squeezing mine and her breathing is in a mess and the sound of it is aching in the top of my head and I'm starting to prickle as if my skin is scared of what will happen to it.

Marilyn sounds the way I've sounded.

I hear the noise of her and expect to breathe in my own breath and smell blood.

That's what used to happen.

There's this rank smell when he makes your nose bleed, like you're a bit rotting, this hot, metal smell of being meat. You still get it the morning after he hits you and for a few days after.

My mum would have been so ashamed that I let him.

And I think I love Marilyn a lot. She was firm with the Tube man, as if she was his gran. She explained us. He asked if we were sure we didn't need any help and Marilyn waved her camping trip water bottle and said she would take a few sips and be fine. And then the man just went away. His face looked surprised with himself and with what he was doing.

I had to make sure I didn't laugh.

Bobby's face just before he got angry was covered in laughter, in smiles. He smiled when he was happy, too, and I wanted to be glad when he was happy, to be happy with him. I was his wife. But you could never tell.

I get things wrong a lot.

Mum made Dad happy and he did that back.

I did, I had a lovely childhood.

You've got no chance after that. You have no idea.

Marilyn has a pack of tissues in her bag and we take one each.

I'm saying to her, 'Bobby didn't do this. I was in a shelter after him and then I was OK. I was kind of OK. This is... I'm someone who went to university.'

She gives me another tissue.

Sensible women everywhere have tissues because they're something you can give. You see a mess or a sadness and you have something you can give.

'The way he hurt me. That's the thing – is the way I am. The way he made it.'

And I can see that she is going to understand me like my mum did and we'll work something out, only the Tube man is here again and he has these two police.

A lady police and a man police.

They're very polite. You know when they do that you're going to be moved on and that the gentleness is there because they can do fuck all to help you. And they're nice, because there are witnesses and maybe not all of them think you deserve whatever comes to you and the hardness and the way it can't be possible, can't be that you're in this and here and can't get out.

I can't believe myself any more, or where I am and how I am, because it's beyond what I can think of. It makes you so slowed-up and stupid.

I get things wrong a lot.

But me and Marilyn, we were sitting in our right place, we were comfortable and friendly. They've spoiled it. She doesn't want me to go. She can see me and think about me and believes that I exist and that's very helpful to me. I would like to point that out.

She wouldn't take me home with her, but she might have, or we could have stayed, stayed here, stayed for hours.

We weren't doing any harm.

She's being angry for me.

I love her very much.

She is shouting and making her accent sound as if they ought to listen. I am proud of her.

They've ruined us, though, and she's wasting her time and bastards are walking by and smiling as if they think she's crazy.

Always there is someone who takes everything away.

I stand up, because when they lean and tower over it means I can't breathe.

I'd made a nice flat, clean and bright walls and only a bit of black mould in the high corners of the bathroom and I treated it with bleach. I was quiet and I took in parcels when people were out and I looked after dogs. I was a good neighbour and people were sorry so sorry to see me go.

The standing makes my legs shake.

The bastards never die and they want you in the wilderness and out you go.

I want to hug her, but my legs are bad and I don't want to fall and we are inside too much of a rush and maybe touching her would be too horrible for her. It might make the police get angry and she might cling on and I might want her to do that.

I am crying at Marilyn and she is crying at me and we are trying to be brave. I think that's what we are doing.

She smells of her own clean warm wash and of a perfume I don't know.

'Sorry. So sorry. So sorry.'

She reaches and grabs my hand for a bit and then I back away and she has to let go. She stands and looks at me after that. She's looking at me but shouting at them and this is going to be the last way I see her, standing under the sign that says Point For Lost Children. She said that meant we ought to be there and I sort of believed her a bit.

I get things wrong.

Are You Part-Something?

Louise Doughty

Just outside the small East Midlands town where I grew up there was a dump, a couple of miles out on the B668, which went by the rather grand title of Civic Amenity Centre – a somewhat fancy name for a place where you took your old armchair. One day in the nineties, my father was up there, getting rid of some household object. He was in his seventies by then, an age when he had a sweep of white hair but a figure still upright and trim on a six-foot-two frame. As he walked away from the dump towards his car, a passing woman in a headscarf stopped and barked at him, 'I say! F'noos 'n' roils!'

He looked at her. 'I beg your pardon, madam?' he asked.

She had a nasal, upper-class manner and a horsey demeanour – not unknown in that area as the surrounding fields were hunting country. She was pointing at his legs. 'F'noos 'n' roils!' she repeated.

My father looked down. He was wearing navy blue tracksuit bottoms with a white stripe down the leg. The penny dropped that the woman was demanding to know if he had served in the Blues and Royals, an army cavalry regiment closely associated with the Royal Family.

'No, madam,' my father replied solemnly, 'Marks & Spencer.'

If you had met my father around this time, you would have thought him a rather upright member of the middle classes, a little upper crust perhaps, with precise manners and pronunciation, something of a pedant for doing things the 'right' way.

And yet, this was also the period in our lives when I, as a newly published author, was becoming prominent enough to give interviews – and he begged me not to talk about our family background.

'I understand why you're interested,' he said, 'but you really should keep quiet, you know. You've got two children to think of.' On one occasion, in 2004, when I had been on *Start the Week* on BBC Radio 4, he said, 'You want to watch it. If you're not careful, you'll get a brick through your window.' Till the end of his days, at the age of eighty-seven, he worried that my talking about my background, by which I mean my ancestral ethnicity, was a threat to my physical safety and that of my family.

'Dad,' I said, with some exasperation, 'who do you think is going to throw a brick through my window?'

'I don't know, those types in Parliament Square, those young men.' He was referring to a recent Countryside Alliance march against the proposed government ban on foxhunting that had ended in scuffles, shown on TV. There was no relationship between those scuffles and our background but what my father had seen, and felt, was a tremor of something he recognised from his youth – right-wing young men on the march, violence.

The woman at the dump mistaking our father for a cavalry officer became a standing joke in our family – for nothing could have been further from the truth. He was the son of a painter and decorator and had left school at thirteen. On his mother's side, his family were English Romanichal Gypsies and, in the working-class area of Peterborough where he grew up during the twenties and thirties, it probably wasn't wise to mention that you had Romany blood, however distant. At that time, my father and his family would have had no idea about the horrors about to be perpetrated against the Roma and Sinti in Europe under Nazi occupation, but prejudice they understood all right, even from within their own family. 'My mother used to hit me when I was bad,' one of my aunts once told me, 'and she always said to me, I'll beat the Gypsy out of you, my girl.' When my father first told me about our family, he asked me not to mention it to neighbours or friends at school – a suggestion guaranteed to create an abiding fascination in the subject for a black-haired, sallow-skinned adolescent growing up in a white rural town who was often asked, 'Are you part-something?' When I gave him a copy of my fourth novel, *Fires in the Dark*, about the Romany Holocaust, he told me, 'I read your book, didn't care for it, wouldn't have finished it if it hadn't been by you.' (My mother later told me he never had finished it.) He always found it hard to accept that, had Germany successfully invaded Britain during the Second World War, he and his family would have qualified for shipping to the gas chambers alongside British Jews.

This would have happened despite our family having been settled since the turn of the twentieth century. In common with many English Romanichals, my ancestors found that the traditional ways of earning a living – horse-dealing, harvesting – came to an end with increasing agricultural mechanisation. At that time, an astute social commentator could have been forgiven for predicting that English Romany culture would rapidly become assimilated into that of the majority population. In 1998, as part of a history programme I made about our family, I asked a Romanichal man at the Barnet Horse Fair what he thought the future of English Travellers was likely to be. 'We're just going to fade away,' he told me. 'It's all going to go.'

In recent years, though, and across Europe, the opposite has been happening. Roma and Sinti people now number between 10 and 12 million and are the fastest growing ethnic minority on the European mainland. Even in the UK, there is an increasingly vocal and visible class of Romany and Traveller activists and intellectuals including the poet David Morley, journalist Jake Bowers, storyteller and playwright Richard Rai O'Neill and artists such as Delaine Le Bas who appeared in the first ever Roma art pavilion at the Venice Biennale. Her son, Damian Le Bas is, as I write this, about to publish *The Stopping Places: A Journey Through Gypsy Britain*, which is featuring as a Radio 4 *Book of the Week*.

Despite this, and the growing politicisation and cross-cultural awareness of many disparate Roma groups, there is no denying that the majority of this huge and various ethnicity live in the most appalling economic conditions, with an estimated 84 per cent across Europe below the recognised poverty line. In this country, the lack of site provision for Travellers has forced many into conflict with local planning regulations and hence straight onto the pages of the tabloids. (The site provision crisis in this country can be traced directly back to 1994 when John Major's government abolished the Caravan Sites Act which obliged local authorities to provide adequate sites for Travellers. At the time, Romanies and Travellers were urged to buy their own land to settle – many duly did, only to find themselves refused planning permission to park their trailers on land which they legally owned.)

As right-wing, anti-immigration movements have grown across Europe, so has anti-Romany prejudice – but in fact, as far as Gypsy, Roma and Traveller people are concerned, it has been happening quietly for decades. Where there is anti-Gypsyism, prejudice against migrancy of all sorts follows as surely as night follows day. We're the canaries in the coalmine. Ten years ago, the British National Party held a Red, White and Blue rally in the village of Denby in Derbyshire and amongst the guests invited to speak was Petra Edelmannová, chair of the Czech National Party, a tiny fringe movement from the Czech Republic notable mainly for its overt antagonism towards the Roma. Edelmannová was invited after publishing a pamphlet entitled 'The Final Solution to the Gypsy Issue in the Czech Lands', which advocated repatriating the Czech Republic's Roma population to India. In the event, Edelmannová didn't show up, but it was an interesting choice of speaker for what the BNP insisted was a weekend of family fun with bouncy castles.

At the time, I interviewed the then-BNP deputy leader Simon Darby for the *Guardian* newspaper. He conceded that the phrase 'final solution' was 'not exactly the best title for a document' but added, 'there is a Gypsy problem there. There is a problem in this country as well.' What did he regard as the nature of our 'Gypsy problem'? 'Some of the Travelling community have been here for a very long time. They keep themselves to themselves and sort out their own problems within their own communities. They have the same morals as me. I don't have a problem with them.' He identified the 'problem' as being foreign Roma who have immigrated into the UK since European enlargement, along with an undefined group of what he calls 'home-grown pseudo-Gypsies'.

This artificial distinction between different groups of Romanies and Travellers in order to justify discrimination was something I also encountered when I spent time in the Czech Republic as a writer in residence at the Masaryk University in Brno. I was told that the problem with the Roma was not 'our Gypsies' but the Slovak Gypsies, many of whose communities moved to the Czech lands to fill labour shortages in factories after the Second World War. The *gadje* (non-Gypsy) world seems to have less of a problem with Romany people as long as they stay in a folkloric pigeonhole and don't grow too numerous – i.e. don't appear to be real people with real housing needs, hunger and educational ambitions for their children.

The invitation extended by the BNP to Petra Edelmannová was significant because the historical treatment of the Roma in the Czech lands provides an instructive example to modern Europe. In more than one European country, the round-up of Roma and Sinti people under Nazi occupation was made that much easier by pre-existing legislation. In Czechoslovakia, as it then was, restrictive legislation against Gypsies was brought in as early as 1927. Law 117 required all Gypsies to be fingerprinted and to provide details of their movements around the country. The evidence gathered under

Law 117 made the internment of Bohemian and Moravian Roma that much easier when the occupying forces of the German army decided the time had come. In August 1942, under the guise of a so-called 'registration day', the Roma and Sinti were rounded up and imprisoned in two camps, Lety in Bohemia and Hodonin in Moravia. After a year, most of the inhabitants of those camps were sent on to Auschwitz where they were murdered. Of the 6,500 Roma in the Czech lands at the start of the war, fewer than 500 survived. What began as fingerprinting in 1927 ended sixteen years later in the gas chambers.

To draw analogies between the Nazi-perpetrated Holocaust and the current situation for European Roma may seem unduly alarmist, but in 1927 anyone who predicted the fate of the Czech lands in the 1940s would have been regarded as alarmist to the point of lunacy. Czechoslovakia was a thriving democracy that had shaken off the shackles of the Austro-Hungarian Empire to emerge as one of the top ten economically developed countries in the world.

The true numbers of Roma and Sinti people murdered by the Nazis will never be known – official estimates vary between one quarter and half a million, although many Romany experts believe a million might be nearer the mark. What is indisputable is that the Roma and Sinti were persecuted to roughly the same proportion of their population, around 85 per cent, as Jewish people – and for the same racial reasons. Where the two genocides differ is that although the Jewish Holocaust was always openly racist, the Roma and Sinti were initially persecuted for being 'asocials', and for many years successive German governments refused to recognise the racial element of the Nazis' actions.

This insistence that the exclusion of and discrimination against Gypsies has more to do with lifestyle than race found its echo in events in Italy that were contemporaneous with that BNP rally. In May 2008, a woman in Ponticelli, outside Naples, reported that a Gypsy woman had attempted to abduct her baby. Whether the report was true or not made no difference to the thugs who descended with iron bars and torches upon local camps and slum housing. The response of the Berlusconi government and its allies was breathtakingly cynical. First came the announcement in June that all Gypsies, children included, would be fingerprinted and, crucially, identified by their ethnicity – a move unprecedented in post-war Western Europe. Terry Davis, the secretary general of the Council of Europe, responded that such a scheme 'invites historical analogies which are so obvious that they do not have to be spelled out'. Even Berlusconi proved sensitive to the international outrage that ensued and the plans were modified. But the rise of nationalistic, anti-migrant politics in Italy has, as it has in many other countries, a clear genesis in anti-Roma measures. Put simply, if you're used to demonising one group of people, you're in the habit, and it's a great deal easier to demonise another.

The slaughter of the Second World War was merely the apotheosis of centuries of persecution throughout the Roma's tragic European history. Although awareness of the Romany Holocaust is now well established, few people know that, for five and a half centuries, thousand of Romanies in Eastern Europe were bought and sold as slaves. According to Professor Ian Hancock in his book, *We Are the Romani People*, 'In the sixteenth century, a Romani child could be purchased for 32p. By the nineteenth century, slaves were sold by weight, at the rate of one gold piece per pound.'

Throughout this history, Roma and Sinti people have traditionally survived by remaining out of sight as much as possible. In Poland, a small number of Polska Roma survived the Nazi genocide by remaining hidden in remote forests. In Bohemia and Moravia, a few families were sheltered by Czech villagers. On a wider level, many Romanies or Travellers simply don't mention their family backgrounds. On a writers' tour of Romania in 2000, one friend said to me, 'I think the attitude of most people here would be, we don't understand why you talk about having Gypsy blood. If you kept quiet about it, you could pass.'

Seen within their Europe-wide and historical context, these attitudes have a devastating effect on the morale of the wider Roma population, not just on those directly victimised – we are, after all, talking about a people who have genocide in living memory and who are amongst the most poverty-stricken and excluded in Europe. New developments are watched across the continent with mounting anxiety and arouse a level of visceral fear amongst Roma and Sinti people that is born of a perfectly justifiable distrust of the *gadje*. For every firebomb thrown into a camp or slum dwelling, for every municipal move to get Romanies to move on, there are a thousand petty incidents of scorn or prejudice. As one English Traveller friend once put it to me, 'Whenever anyone says to me, oh it must be so romantic being a Gypsy, I say, what's romantic about being spat at?'

Most Roma live in such poverty that their choices are severely curtailed: the immigrant Roma in Italy are there because they left countries such as Romania in search of better lives. Travellers turned off the land they own in Cambridgeshire or Essex are forced to camp by the side of the road or on publicly owned recreation grounds. However often the Romany and Traveller communities of Europe are moved on, from borough to borough or across national boundaries, they will not be fading away or melting into thin air. Until there is pan-European political will to address the poverty and exclusion that many face, the situation can only worsen, and the right wing will continue to use this marginalised group, as they do many others, as a vote-scoring chip.

My father died in 2012 and went to his grave with feelings of profound ambivalence towards his background: proud of the achievements of his children (all three of us were the first generation in either our mother or father's families to go to university) but concerned that my pride in his origins would lead to discrimination. Although I gently mocked his concern about bricks through windows, I never had the courage to confirm his concern by telling him of some of the comments I get online when I talk about my ancestry. At my father's eightieth birthday party, I told my aunt about his remark about the bricks, expecting her to agree with me that my father was an incorrigible worrier. Instead, she said quietly, 'He's got a point, love, hasn't he?'

The A–Z of an Earthquake Zone

Kamila Shamsie

Kashmir, December 2006

AFTERMATH:

Everything here is aftermath.

BAGH:

The city's name means 'garden', but nothing grows in rubble. You must piece together clues – a doorframe in the middle of a field, an open-air restaurant that wasn't previously open-air – to imagine this place as it must have been two months ago, before the earthquake struck. Prior to coming here, I had been looking at pictures of World War II and now, driving through Bagh, I recall pictures of Dresden, of Nagasaki.

CHILDREN:

They make up 70 per cent of the dead. Not because they are weaker, less capable of withstanding falling beams or knowing how to seek safety, but because every government school in the area collapsed, even when the buildings around it remained intact. But everywhere you go, especially if you have a camera, the children – the survivors – come to find you with smiles that make you believe they are entirely resilient; then you hear the District Education officer say they are terrified by the stirring of the breeze.

DISTRIBUTION:

Much of the relief work I'm involved with in my week at Sungi, an NGO in Muzaffarabad, consists of helping distribute the materials to build a house – corrugated sheets, nails, tarps, shovels, wire, etc. – to those whose homes have 'totally collapsed'. My initial role is filling out coupons with people's names and their villages; those coupons are later exchanged for housing materials. It is something anyone with basic literacy skills could do. It is also the most significant writing of my life.

ESTIMATES:

The official number of the dead hovers around 75,000. Everyone here says the figure is ridiculously low. A hundred and fifty thousand is the minimum estimate. Three hundred thousand is not considered too outrageous a suggestion.

FAIRY TALES:

– 'In the first days after the earthquake it was frightening to go out. You never knew what you'd see. Some things you heard were straight out of fairy tales. There was a schoolboy thrown into the air by the force of the quake. Two of his friends caught hold of his kameez to pull him down, but they were carried up with him. All three of them, carried up into the mountain. Their parents rushed to the school to see if they were still alive, but those three boys – who had been in that schoolyard with the rest of the students – were nowhere to be seen. They appeared a long time later; it had taken them a while to come down from the mountain.'

GOD:

– 'Everything has turned upside. There are rivers where before the land was dry, barren land where once there were rivers. The most religious of men have turned away from God, and those who were interested only in their own pleasure now spend all day in prayer.'

What is most turned around, to my way of thinking, is these people who've suffered so much casting themselves in the role of perpetrator rather than victim. God is punishing us, I hear repeatedly. This happened because we brought it upon ourselves.

– 'And the children? What were their crimes?' I ask one man.

– 'As far as the children are concerned... I think God has wronged them terribly.'

HEROISM:

Every destination is further than it should be. Roads have slid off mountainsides, bridges are collapsed, straight tracks have become steep inclines. Sajjad, one of the Sungi workers I'm out in the field with, points to a bridge and says he was in the first vehicle to cross the bridge after the earthquake. Everyone else was scared it would collapse, but it was necessary to get to the people on the other side. He says this with a shrug, as though those who refused to go across were being needlessly cautious. But I look into the deep drop beneath as we cross the wooden bridge, each plank clattering beneath the wheels, and I know I'm sitting next to a hero.

IZHAR:

– 'There has always been suffering,' says Izhar the headmaster. 'The prophets, most pious of all, had to bear it. Look at Moses, look at Noah. What has changed between then and now is that now we have relief workers.'

Not enough, I think. Not nearly as many as helped with the tsunami. This is what I've learned from reading the foreign press: how poorly we've been aided by comparison. But Izhar, like all the other Kashmiris I meet, sees it differently.

– 'What I've learned is that humanity's pain is humanity's pain. It's not surprising that other Muslims came to our aid, but look at how many non-Muslims also came. And during Ramzan they would refuse to eat in front of us, even though we said that wasn't necessary. They weren't the ones fasting – why should they go hungry? But they wouldn't eat, they wouldn't even smoke their cigarettes.'

JOLTS:

I'm sitting in the Sungi office, when I feel the room shake as though someone has angrily slammed a door. My first aftershock – there have been over a thousand since the earthquake – and I stop to imagine what might have happened if it had occurred earlier in the day while I was walking along a narrow winding mountain path to reach a village inaccessible by road.

KASHMIR:

A word to conjure with. At the start of my week, as the van filled with volunteer relief workers turned a bend and Muzaffarabad lay in front of us, one of the boys in the van told the driver to stop so we could all get out and look at the place of rhetoric become mountain and valley and river.

– 'If you were a poet, you'd write about this,' says one of the boys. Then he adds, 'But really there are very few poets. Faraz, Iqbal – those are poets. The rest who write their little verses, they aren't poets, just lovers.'

I text a friend in Huddersfield: It is absurdly beautiful. It must be easy for such a place to drive young men to poetry or death.

LANGUAGE:

– '*Voh dub gaee*,' a woman says of her seven-year-old daughter.

Voh dub gaee, a common enough Urdu expression. But I've only ever heard it used figuratively, indicating a complete loss of spirit. Suddenly here it is the literal truth. *Voh dub gaee*. She was flattened.

MUJAHIDEEN:

– 'They came down from the mountains almost immediately. These men who we always knew existed, but had never seen. They came with their satellite phones, their SUVs and their extraordinary organisation. They pulled so many people out of the rubble – and corpses, too; they would go and recover dead bodies from places no one else wanted to go near.'

– 'What about the army?'

– 'The thing about the army is they lost thousands of their own in the earthquake. So they were frantic getting their injured to hospital, recovering the bodies of their dead. They were in no state then to help anyone else. No, it was the mujahideen who were here first. You know, there was this American journalist covering the relief effort, who wanted to know about the mujahideen. She kept trying to get me to use the word 'terrorist' or 'militant' and I finally had to say, "This is your language. Here people have always thought of them as freedom fighters."'

NOISE:

– 'The screaming. I'll never forget the screaming.'

– 'The screaming? Of the people trapped by the earthquake?'

– 'No, of the earth splitting and the mountains falling.'

OCTOBER 8:

There were about seven seconds during which the vast bulk of the destruction took place. Imagine those seven seconds, I am repeatedly told. I can't.

PAKISTAN:

In Karachi, everyone says this is the first time in people's memories that the nation has truly banded together, without concern for ethnicity or religious affiliation or tribal divide or political differences. But up in Azad Kashmir – Free Kashmir, as Pakistanis call it to differentiate it from 'Indian-Occupied Kashmir' – one of the locals, on hearing I'm from Karachi, smiles with genuine warmth and says, 'You Pakistanis have done more for us than any other nation.'

QUEUING:

I have never witnessed such a thing before. In the villages around Muzaffarabad, they queue for their coupons, their blankets, their corrugated sheets. There are no policeman or army officers standing to a side with batons or guns – and yet they queue. Silently. Patiently. You'd think this was Wimbledon, you'd think they were English. It disturbs me unaccountably.

Then I'm told it wasn't like this a month or two ago. Then, distribution trucks would be swarmed – sometimes attacked – by the needy and the desperate. So yes, this is a good thing – there is a system in place, and people have learned to trust to it. Everyone who has been here since the earthquake says an incredible amount has been achieved; it's important not to be overwhelmed by the work that remains to be done, and to also take time to appreciate what has been done.

All this is true. But the silence of the queues makes me wonder if I'm witnessing a flattening of the spirit.

RELIEF, REHABILITATION, RECONSTRUCTION:

Two months after the fact, you'd think the RELIEF phase would be over. And it's true that things are moving on to the next two Rs.

But my second day in Kashmir, I find myself in the mountains, talking to villagers who say there's been no aid since the military helicopters airlifted the most seriously wounded and left twenty tents for three villages. There are ten to twelve families living in each tent and last night, during the first snowfall, most of the tents collapsed. I ask one of the women in the village if there's a food shortage.

– 'It isn't a shortage. There's no food.'

It's the middle of the afternoon, the warmest part of the day: I'm wearing several layers of clothing, two pairs of wool socks and winter boots and I'm freezing. This is only the very beginning of winter.

SUNGI:

– 'We were like children who, on the day of a massive storm, go down to the sea and say, come on, let's learn to sail.'

So Uzma Gul, the Sungi co-ordinator at Muzaffarabad, describes Sungi's immersion in relief work in the immediate aftermath of the earthquake; as a local NGO with offices and contacts in the very heart of the affected areas, Sungi was ideally placed to take part in the relief efforts. The only problem, as Uzma points out, is that Sungi is an NGO that works for the rights of the marginalised; relief work had only ever played a very tiny part in its operations. But the earthquake left no room for bystanders. The only option was to throw yourself into the storm, and learn to sail.

By the time I arrive in Muzaffarabad, everyone in the office has found their sea-legs – and stamina. They start work by 8.30, are out in the field until sunset, and don't leave the office until after midnight.

– 'After this, returning to a normal nine-to-five day will feel like being on holiday,' Uzma says.

– 'And when do you think that will happen?'

– 'Around June.'

TENT-VILLAGES:

On every empty plot of land, there are tent-villages. Each one with the flags of a different country, or NGO, or political party. I imagine looking down from one of the helicopters that fly past every few minutes; it must look like a board game. Risk, With a Heart.

But for all those who have come to the tent-villages, there are thousands who remain without shelter in the places where their homes once stood. Those who've lost – or never had – property papers know their presence is the only thing that will guarantee their continued ownership of their land. Those whose only income is livestock must stay up in the mountains with their goats and cows, for whom there is no space in these cramped tent-villages.

– 'Can't anything be done to convince them to come down?'

– 'The cold will convince them soon enough.'

UNDERLAY:

The mountains look strange. Vast strips of grey all along them, as though someone forgot to put pine-and-mud carpet over the underlay. Those are landslides. And that rubble over there, which

I imagine must be a flattened house, is the remnant of a five-storey hotel, the grandest in Muzaffarabad.

VISTAS:

Despite everything, there are times you forget why you are there, what has happened. You watch the sun glide down the mountains into the valleys which are intersected by fleet rivers in whose waters women wash brightly coloured clothes and you just stand there, looking down, thinking, how beautiful.

WOMEN:

It's bad enough for the men. But for the women in the tent-cities there is also the increased risk of sexual assault, the problems arising from a lack of privacy, the hygiene issues. The widows rely on male relatives to act as their proxies at distribution sites. Their state of dependence is terrifying. If they had nothing to cope with but their grief, that in itself would be too much.

X, Y, Z:

The alphabet's close, the final stages, the announcement of an ending. If only that were true. But there is still so much rubble and so many children whose absences will be a constant presence for those who survive – not just in Kashmir, but in too many parts of the world.

Living in a Country of Words: The Shelter of Stories

Marina Warner

In April 2018, around eighty young refugees and asylum seekers (*minorenni*, or minors, aged eighteen and under) were taking part in the project Stories in Transit in Palermo. The plan was to set out from Ballarò, the old multicultural part of the city, and go for a walk through the historic centre, where many of them hadn't been before – not because it is forbidden to them, but for other reasons arising from their situation: they don't want to run any more risks now that they have crossed the Mediterranean and found shelter (temporarily) in Italy. The centre of Palermo still carries the scars of heavy bombing in World War II, and the sights of the wreckage beside the busy markets and crowded streets might inspire a sympathetic connection between the Sicilian past and these young people, who have fled violence of every kind. We divided up into bands, supplied the *minorenni* with blank drawing pads and pencils, and urged them to set down things they saw or heard or smelled, recognised or discovered in any way they wanted – sketches, writing, etc. 'I don't know how to draw!' one protested. 'No matter, just do what you can, just to remember what you find as we go,' we responded.

The idea was to gather sights and sounds towards making story maps and thereby shape a sense of ownership for young people who have mostly arrived alone and left behind everything they know. Our first destination was a strange Renaissance statue in a ruined square: an old bearded king sitting on a throne with a very large snake wound around his legs and rising up to nurse at his breast. He's the city's mascot, known as the Genius of Palermo, and reappears in different forms here and there in the town's squares and streets; our final meeting point was a fountain on which he stands, looking up at the sky – in hope, for this is the Piazza Rivoluzione and records the end of Spanish rule in Sicily.

The young men and women took to the task with a will and the tourists and citizens wondered at them without any antagonism: it is amazing what a difference it makes to carry a drawing pad and start looking carefully at everything around, noting things down. People were curious, in a friendly way, and admiring of the results. One local came out of his house with an old photograph of the square to show us what it looked like before the war. One of the *minorenni*, Amadou, who comes from Guinea, began outlining the meaning of the mysterious king with his snake: the creature was not venomous, he declared, but most people mistook its nature.

Stories in Transit began in 2016, and the project proceeds on the principle that arrivants have a right to cultural expression (arrivant is the more open, factual, and welcoming term Kamau Brathwaite adopted in his epic, *The Arrivants: A New World Trilogy* – the term embraces immigrant, émigré, migrant, refugee, asylum seeker, etc.). Such new arrivals are often severed from families and friends and from their geography of home, and one of their needs that should command attention is the need for culture. Culture will develop spontaneously, of course; music, confabulation, art, and so on cannot be altogether stifled. Yet creating conditions for expressions and exchanges to happen remains vital, even when other resources are extremely stretched. Stories in Transit encourages displaced individuals to tell stories, drawing on their own traditions and their faculty of imagination. We then workshop the material together, in combinations of media – puppetry, animation, performance – with movement and music, without relying too deeply on language (we can't yet all communicate with one another, since their Italian is in its early stages, and they come from all over Africa and the Middle East).

The project grew out of four key issues which we explored in the initial stages, in Palermo and in Oxford:[1]

1. Can culture, and specifically storytelling in every form of narrative expression, provide a kind of shelter for people who have lost their homes? Can a tale become a home? A *lieu de mémoire*? Can a memory of literature and the process of making it over and over again build 'a country of words', to quote a famous poem by Mahmoud Darwish?[2] Can narratives build a place of belonging for those without a nation?

2. In times of great physical deprivation, the argument needs to be made for the right of access to a life of the mind and creative potential. It is all too frequent that culture, including education in the arts and humanities, is set aside, regarded as a luxury.

What cultural steps can be taken to affirm the right of arrivants to freedom of thought and imagination – intellectual mobility? Is expressing the imagination and passing on traditions and testimony part of human rights?

3. What methods and processes can be developed together to allow the unfolding and generation of stories? What role can imaginary, mythic narratives play in contemporary conditions? In what ways can the ancient human capacity to tell and pass on stories help in the present crisis? Can make-believe help make-truth?

4. What are the best uses of contemporary media for supporting exchanges of stories across borders and easing communications between languages and cultures?

In my own fiction and essays, I have written about flight, about the loss of home and the loss of bearings, and the recent intensity of the refugee situation made me feel quite helpless to do anything, as it does us all. I was looking at images of camps with their endless rows of tents or huts, and no focal points or gathering places, and wondering how these new cities – many of the inhabitants spend decades living there – could be given some qualities of home.[3] In my 2015 Holberg Lecture I explored the question of literature as an alternative shelter. Then I noticed, from a drawing published by Save the Children, that a refugee child named Farah had drawn a crowd around... the lorry delivering water. Like the water sources and laundries where news and stories used to be exchanged, like the magic wells in so many fairy tales where encounters take place and carry the characters over into another dimension of reality, the water supply created a place of exchange and fellowship. It strikes me as beautiful and profoundly right that the Arabic verb *rawaa* means both 'to water' or 'to irrigate' and 'to relate' and that a *raawi* is a transmitter of poetry. As the comparative literature scholar and Arabist Philip Kennedy comments, '*Rawwii* is well-watered; there are lots of versions of the root, including *riwaaya* which now means a story (or novel).'[4]

The Country of Words

In 1931 the philosopher Alfred Korzybski coined a crisp and pungent phrase: 'The map is not the territory.'[5] A map does not chart the territory as it is recorded by an ordnance surveyor but territory as it is experienced by someone on the ground, whatever its actual measurable facts; it is a story, if you like, not a factual history. Korzybski was talking in terms of neurolinguistics and pointing out how our perceptions and beliefs as individuals and members of a society are gathered over time and constitute our/their reality. 'We are the story we tell' has become a cliché, but I think it has profound significance, especially in times of violent uprootings and horrendous losses – at every level, literal and figurative. However, this mode of reattaching oneself to a place that is not home but must become one does not necessarily depend on transmitting an existing story. Nor does it depend on inheriting a national myth or story through historical or geographic bonds. It can evolve through mutual exchanges and invention: it can dream and speculate and comment and even laugh.

Displaced individuals and peoples, like the tens of thousands now fleeing wars and drought, can find a place of belonging in an immaterial zone where the 'intangible goods' of culture, as UNESCO terms them, are remembered and revisioned (these include ballads, nursery rhymes and lullabies as well as the common imagery of artifacts, vessels and tools and furnishings – carpets are carriers of stories, too). Darwish's poem later alludes to elements that for him help construct the country of words – the Psalms, gypsy lore, the *Arabian Nights* – and to these echoes and reflections one could add much wonderful verbal baggage, ancient and close to us in time, eclectic and far-flung as well as local. *The Epic of Gilgamesh*, the earliest and one of the most stirring sequences of stories ever composed, is still growing and changing, as more tablets are unearthed and discovered. Yet this most enduring of imaginative artifacts slept for thousands of years, buried, opaque, and unread, until 1872, when cuneiform was deciphered by George Smith, working in the Assyriology Department of the British Museum. The poem had travelled in pieces, it had waited centuries to be reassembled, and it has continued to shape-shift since into many new forms. It is a travelling tale, like so many others.[6]

Recently, the Algerian artist Katia Kameli filmed a traditional storyteller who regularly performs in the famous square in Marrakesh, the Djemaa el-Fna, reciting a tale from his repertoire. Every inch the timeless figure of a *hakawati* or griot, grey-haired and gaunt in a djellaba against a backdrop of a ruinous building, Abderrahim al-Azalia spins a marvellous romance of love and obstacles, wonders and triumphs. Throughout this traditional recitation, Kameli has intercut clips from a Bollywood film, *Dosti*

(1964), revealing the source of a seemingly authentic tale from Morocco, which has in fact wandered around the world and back again and is now going forth once more to new listeners, who will transform it and carry it further.

In relation to the nomadic and metamorphic character of stories, there is a delightful and profound *récit* by the Moroccan scholar and fabulist Abdelfattah Kilito. Called *Métaphore*, it pictures the Arabic ode (the pre-Islamic form at the foundations of Arabic composition) as an orphaned she-camel who goes wandering about the desert until someone adopts her. Kilito, who has commented richly on travelling texts such as the Bible and the *Arabian Nights*, sees himself above all as a porter, a story-bearer, like one of the many such characters in the *Nights*. *Métaphore* begins, 'The ode, said the poets in former times, is a stray she-camel: you don't know where she'll end up.' (I think one can widen 'ode' to apply to literature and stories, though poetry is easier to memorise and so can travel more swiftly.) Kilito goes on:

> Lost in the immensity of the desert, she [the camel-ode] wanders looking for her nearest and dearest, animal and human. But it's not certain that she'll find them again. One day or other, the orphan will be taken in by persons unknown, who'll adopt her, and she'll spend the rest of her days among them.
>
> Unless she wanders off again.
>
> Isn't it the fate of an ode to wander, to be a stranger everywhere?

This was something known to the Arab poet of the desert. But he thought that his odes would never be read other than in Arabic. He was far from grasping that his she-camels, centuries later, would have reached towns of which he had not the slightest idea: Berlin, Paris, London, New York.

Translated, interpreted, accompanied by commentaries, they now speak in foreign tongues.

With time, they'll doubtless forget the idiom of their original.[7]

In another part of the world, Ireland, during the 1970s when the Troubles were acute, some writers began publishing a magazine called *The Crane Bag*. The title comes from an eerie Irish myth that Aoife, the wife of the God of the Sea, stole from him the secret of writing; for this she was magically changed into a crane, a bird whose flight is a kind of sky writing, thought to be the origin of the alphabet itself. The God of the Sea then took the skin of his wife and made it into a fishing net – the crane bag – and kept all his treasures in it, including writing. The magazine, which took the name of this magical instrument, was dedicated to the imagination. In a foreword, Seamus Heaney wrote a kind of manifesto for literature as a way of participating in society and history through acts of imagination: 'A mind [so] stretched between transcendence and politics produces exactly the kind of fibre from which this trawl-net of the mind is to be rewoven'.[8]

Since that time, the kinds of violence that convulsed Ireland are occurring in many places with a ferocity that inspires a feeling of utter despair. Is there anything writers can do? What can culture achieve?

Recent developments in literary criticism have begun to explore the human mind according to the methods of cognitive studies, and the findings reinforce Heaney's call for engagement through imagination. Terence Cave writes in *Thinking with Literature*:

> Human cognition is alert, attentive, responsive. Above all, it is *imaginative*: it can think beyond the constraints of immediate experience, do strange things with words, conjure up futures and histories of all kinds, bring to life people who never existed and invent for them plausible stories and environments. Despite the tangible evidence that this is so, the word 'cognition' has traditionally been used to refer to the rational knowledge-seeking processes of the mind as opposed to other modes of engagement with the world.[9]

Memory and imagination have been considered faculties apart, enclosed in different physical parts of the head; only Leonardo da Vinci intuited, in a drawing of the cross-section of the brain, how intertwined they are.[10] Neuroscientists have now discovered that when we conjure up a hypothetical scene (as in writing fiction), we use the same mental regions as when we remember something that happened to us.

With regard to people on the move, their stories are key to their success as asylum seekers, but the dominant form of storytelling that arrivants are encouraged to adopt is autobiographical, and their legal situation requires them to tell this story in a way that will meet the regulations for asylum; this *récit*, or account, resembles the pardon tales that past condemned criminals were permitted to write to the king in France to sue for grace. Natalie Zemon Davis, in her illuminating study *Fiction in the Archives*, shows dramatically how only the author of the most effective story would succeed in capturing the ruler's attention and receiving amnesty. The way the story was told weighed more than the content; the more dramatic and the more heartfelt, the stronger the chances of success. In early modern Europe the subject seeking pardon told his or her story once, in this crucial epistle to the powers above; a refugee today must tell it again and again and never deviate from the circumstances as given from the first moment. The story can become a mark of identity that becomes a yoke, an insurmountable border in itself: you must not change your story.

The pardon tale has counterparts that have even greater currency in contemporary culture: the slave narrative, the psychological confession shaped by the quest for trauma and its causes, and the witness statement before the Truth and Reconciliation Commission. An act of testimony, such as Kate Drumgoold's in *A Slave Girl's Story* (1898), brings into our ears across the years the singular and powerful voice of an individual, remembering what happened to her. Her story, like more famous accounts such as Olaudah Equiano's, are overwhelming documents of historical witness; they are narratives in which sincerity and authenticity are of paramount importance. They strike us as true, and it is crucial that they do so. Confession, as in South Africa before the Truth and Reconciliation Commission, also presupposes deep commitment to truthfulness; but although psychoanalysis also digs into what happened in the past to shape or help the individual in the present, the process also generally allows the analysand the benefit of the doubt: truth is what appears to be true to the one who remembers and revisits the event. In this respect, psychoanalysis allows the subject to be unreliable. This understanding does not extend to arrivants or refugees or migrants anywhere.

Legal entry requirements rely on forensic forms of narrative, truth-telling in the first person. I am not directly criticising lawyers or even immigration officers and border agents for obeying these principles. The press, as well as thousands of well-wishers, also encourage the retelling of the personal story, the originary tale of that individual's coming: epic odysseys, testimony that remembers and communicates cruelty and terrible suffering. We listen helplessly, trying to feel – to *empathise* – and sometimes feeling that the emotions that the stories stir are helping us to do something. However, in relation to the well-being of the individuals caught up in these massive upheavals and dislocations, these forms of narrative restrict the human spirit to a single genre of narrative and, I believe, narrow the potential for flourishing through imaginative engagement with the world.

This emphasis on testifying can add another loss: the loss of a shared culture, both from the past place of belonging and in the new places of arrival. The witness statement, the confession, the traumatic utterance of memory all depend on the subject's own lived experience, not on dreamed or imagined possibilities. Fantasy is intrinsically disadvantaged, and that continual interplay between memory and imagination is denied. The single-subject narrative, what the Dutch call the ego-document, is in itself restrictive and a conventional form: most tellers of these tales present themselves as integers, obeying the tradition of the genre, which requires them to present themselves as such, rather than as kindred spirits in a group. (Refugee families may be treated as exceptions to this expectation.)

Yet the long history of storytelling includes myriad alternative ways of shaping experience into narrative, and the most ancient cultures, Eastern and Western, have wrought some of the most wonderful expressions of courage, hope, resistance, and yes, resilience in these modes. For both the host communities where the displaced people arrive and for the arrivants themselves, a space for these other ways of telling stories can inaugurate and stitch and invigorate relations between strangers. Such genres include tall tales, proverbs, jokes, riddles, satire, romances, tales of wonder and magic, fairy tales, animal fables, ballads, song lyrics and, above all perhaps, those supremely unlikely stories, myths. Reflecting on such stories as Odysseus' encounters with the goddess Athena or the metamorphoses of young men and women into flowers, mountains, springs, and trees, one Latin author commented, 'These things never happened but always are.' This was Sallustius, in *Concerning the Gods and the Universe* – not a very widely read text these days.[11] He could have added many other stories, ones explaining the origin of phenomena and probing the extremes of human passion and sorrow. The stories' internal narrators may be nameless or famous: Ulysses, Helen of Troy, Sindbad. Their external authors are sometimes mythical themselves

(Homer or Shahrazad) or the most thought-provoking messengers of knowledge about human existence (Aeschylus, Virgil, Nezami). Not one of them writes autobiography.

Process, Not Product

The Stories in Transit project has held a series of workshops since 2016 (see the website storiesintransit.org). After the first visit to Palermo, with the support of Dr Clelia Bartoli, a civil rights lawyer at the University of Palermo, and Dr Valentina Castagna, a lecturer in English literature and a translator (also at the University of Palermo), a group of the young participants formed themselves into a cooperative called Giocherenda, from a Fula word meaning cooperation, negotiation, unity.[12] They began making storytelling toys and tools – dice, cards, a wheel of fortune – and have established an Etsy shop online and a busy diary of engagements at fairs and festivals all over the island. This is a splendid and successful initiative, which has won local funding and interest from the EU, and it continues the process that lies at the heart of Stories in Transit: to open lines of communication and create ties among the arrivants themselves and with the town and its inhabitants, and to enjoy making up stories – incidentally a form of activity that does not rob anyone else of a job.

In November 2017, the project returned for a full workshop to involve as many young people as we could in a puppet promenade play inspired by *The Epic of Gilgamesh* and the work of making music, masks, scenes, etc. The deeper aim has been all along to give space to imagination and play, in the sense of invention, improvisation, enjoyable expressivity. This hope evolved in discussion in London in September, with the theatre director Mercedes Kemp suggesting the format from her previous experience.

The *nessi* (Italian for 'links', a word the project has adopted in preference to the heavier sounding 'facilitator') came mostly from UK and Italy, and our areas of interest and our practices covered some of the skills needed: theatre, music, object-making, scene-making, etc.[13]

Around eighty *minorenni* joined us after school on 16 November 2017. We played various warming-up games: tossing a ball to each speaker and thereby creating a web of wool as we each gave our names, for example. In another, when each of us was asked to think of a place we felt attached to, the young people almost all gave the name of a place they hope to go to... Oslo, Stockholm, Canada. When one *ragazzo* – I think Oska from Congo – said 'Zabrata', there were gales of laughter (Zabrata is in Libya, a place where they have all suffered horribly, but the gallows humour was shared by all). Mercedes led a round of passing a squeeze from hand to hand... we began very slowly but she spurred us on, after several tries, to manage the circle in fifteen seconds.

Yousif Latif Jaralla, who originally fled the war in Iraq and arrived in Sicily in the nineties, performed a version of *Gilgamesh*, partly supported by Dine Diallo. He had performed it for us before, and this time he included the episode of the Flood, and laid emphasis on the various battles – between Gilgamesh and Enkidu, between the two heroes and Humbaba. Yousif's storytelling reverberated with the young people's experiences, and set the scene quite closely for the story as it was taken up in the play.

After lunch, Dine Diallo and Gassimou Magassouba of the Giocherenda group led a workshop on creating a character. They had been collaborating on devising this with the poet Steve Willey the weekend before, when he had gone out specially to prepare the way. They gave us large pieces of paper with diagrams of the features of Enkidu – his mouth, ears, mouth eyes, etc. – and also his body. We split up into five groups and were all invited to contribute responses, which were then to be assembled into five distinct Enkidus. We exchanged all the notions that had come up – which included eyes that shot flame, half fingers from so many fights, and ears that flapped – and tried to combine them. It was hugely entertaining as well as useful, and I think really led the way to us cohering as a band of people all intent on making something together and passing it on to others. The discussion and exchanges sparked masses of experimental fun with the masks and giant puppets of Gilgamesh, Enkidu and Humbaba. As a result, the Enkidu figure turned out very carnival-like and festive, with a mobile tongue, a blue nose (from the packing of a fruit box) and webbed feet.

After this, we split up into groups and tasks and each group picked an episode to concentrate on. We decided on five scenes from the *Epic*, broadly speaking.

Lee Shearman set up his animation table and began working on showing the young people how to articulate silhouette puppets for stop-frame filming. Several were attracted and kept very busy and focused. I went to the suburbs with Dine and Maria to buy wood and collect the saw and other tools from the Centro Arrupe, where Giocherenda has been given a room for its work by this Jesuit establishment (there are no more priests, but excellent staff and lovely premises). The process continued on Friday and Saturday: Stevie Wishart, Alice Oswald and Phil Terry went upstairs to a closed room with the musicians, who were playing the violins we had brought with us. Other *nessi* – Peter Oswald and Wafa Tarnowska – were involving more young people, including Ismail, Keita, Omar, Ibrahim and Gibril, and worked with them in the courtyard on the representation of the journey across the sea to see Utnapishtim, the last survivor of the Great Deluge. David Swift and I set up tables and with several young people took up the puppets made in May and began refreshing them. When the young people went to Friday prayers, we went to reconnoitre the *Orto Botanico* (Botanical Garden), and Mercedes was able to choose the setting for the different scenes, at stations on the way under the lush foliage and flowering trees.

Sunday 19 November opened with a terrific thunderstorm, so we were worried that the puppets and the splendid boat the group had made with Peter and Wafa would be destroyed; they were too big to fit in anyone's car. But the sky cleared suddenly and the wind dropped, and when we reached the *Orto Botanico*, birds were singing madly with joy at being so deliciously bathed, and the leaves on the trees and plants shone in their newly washed freshness and the light was entirely beautiful, the colours of the greens and yellows bright and vigorous, and the whole marvellous place felt like Eden.

There was great confusion to begin with – some of the young musicians hadn't turned up (several of the refugees do voluntary work helping old people with their shopping, etc.). But eventually the band was gathered together and set up in two answering choruses across a stretch of the garden, and the performance began. All scenes were accompanied by music – rhythm and percussion, mainly strings and drums, and the crowd was given maracas-like eggs to shake and other instruments to beat and blow.

We then moved on to the primary school Ferrara in Piazza Magione and repeated the sequence in the forecourt, which was set with stools for the children, and decking under the shade trees, making for natural stages. There was a large audience here, as the school was holding a festival: many small children and their parents. One little girl, aged around seven or eight, said to me, 'That isn't a plant of immortal life. It's an artichoke!' Her mother responded, '*Tesoro*, artichokes are a bud, you see, and they open up into something else, so they can give a sense of hope.'

We then walked on through the town to the Museo Internazionale Pasqualino delle Marionette – about fifteen minutes away. The young men carried the boat and the puppets to the sound of drums and sticks, singing one of their own songs as they walked. Nobody stopped us or gave us disapproving looks. We reached the museum, where the benches in the theatre upstairs had been set in a large circle. Two of the young people who had been trying out puppetry with Yousif and the *puparo* (puppeteer) Carmelo Mimmo Cuticchio showed us a scene between Angelica and Charlemagne, while the young woman Hajar recited the story. Then we adjourned to the exhibition space next to the theatre as it can be darkened, in order to see a projection of the animation film made by several young arrivants, guided by Lee. This dramatised very vividly Gilgamesh under the sea, with a particularly successful close-up articulated figure of his hand picking the plant, to a musical score.

Many *nessi* had comments and criticisms, but there was general elation that so many of the young arrivants had taken part with such enthusiasm and interest, and that the rough and ready performance was so well received, in spite of all the constraints.

As I write, the Minister of the Interior, from the right-wing Lega party who are part of the new government in Italy, has closed the ports and a rescue boat with over 600 refugees on board is stranded in the Mediterranean. The atmosphere in Palermo will have changed, and the mood will be more sombre, to say the least. We shall be returning for a workshop from 25–30 September, and we were expecting there to be a new group of arrivants entering the refugee schools. But if those who have fled their homes can't enter Italy, they will find somewhere else, and political promises to deport them back are just so much wasted breath – like Trump's Mexican wall. The movement of peoples is a modern reality and realistic modes need to develop to allow its potential to flower (the past gives us many examples – the USA's own history, above all).

We shall be developing an animated film inspired by a story, 'The Huntsman and the King's Son', which Dine Diallo remembers his grandfather telling him in Guinea; we are returning to work on the puppet promenade play of *The Epic of Gilgamesh*; and we are also picking up the thread of the story behind the Genius and his serpent offspring, in the form of a *kavaad*, or folding box with painted scenes, which traditional travelling storytellers use in the Punjab in India to illustrate the unfolding episodes of their narratives.

The future needs to be discussed: we are still aiming at handing over the project to the young people themselves, under the aegis of Giocherenda, and we have been offered an exhibition in the new Project Space at the Hayward Gallery, London, in January 2020. But the situation of the participants is of course unknown, and it would be a disgrace if none of them could be there, for the exhibition and workshops, because they have been refused visas to enter the UK.

Stars

Gillian Allnutt

There are those who have not fled shame
the numberlessness of *am*
the innumerable one

in whom

the dark of the moon, as absence, abstinence, is home.
In shoals, in sheols, they will come
with mobile phones.

Shalom.

An August night, clear and dark, in the Golden Valley near the Anglo-Welsh border – and I notice the stars and the number and anonymity of them.

Though it is 2014 and still a year before refugees from Africa and the Middle East will begin arriving on the shores of Greece and Italy in sufficient numbers to become a 'crisis' in the mind of Europe, I have already worked for two or three years with asylum seekers in the North East of England. I've had a chance to think about what it means to work with people who arrive in the UK usually with very little other than the human ways of the more traditional and spiritual societies they have come from and the suffering they have undergone – and a mobile phone. I've thought a lot about how they've fed my hunger for the spiritual in the bland and pleasant land of the UK in which we find ourselves today and about how grateful I am for that. And I've thought about how I had to learn to use my mobile phone in order, sometimes, to communicate with them and about how grateful I am for that too.

I have been thinking about anonymity for a long time. For me, it can have a positive or a negative value. It can be as nameless as an asylum seeker or a refugee or an economic migrant, not speaking my language, not knowing my ways and inspiring me with fear, especially if it comes in a great crowd. Or it can be as nameless – paradoxically – as the deepest, most intimate place in myself, the place I almost never reach in meditation, the place I think the poet Yeats meant in his phrase 'the deep heart's core'. Anonymity is both the place before and the place after individuality, individualism, the place of the selfie. As the place after it can be full of joy and beautiful.

And three more things.

Shame: I suspect that if you have not known shame then you will not have known the give and take of love.

Sheol *is the Hebrew name of the land of the dead. It's not like hell, it's more like the Ancient Greek idea of where the dead go, being dark and cold and full of shadows, and you can't come back from it. I have heard it suggested that* Sheol *is a metaphor for life on earth, that it is here and now.*

Shalom *means 'Peace' or 'Peace be with you' and is again a Hebrew word.*

A Deep and Persistent Shame

Noam Chomsky

In some countries, there is a real refugee crisis. In Lebanon, for example, where perhaps one-quarter of the population consists of refugees from Syria, over and above a flood of refugees from Palestine and Iraq. Other poor and strife-ridden countries of the region have also absorbed huge numbers of refugees, among them Jordan, and Syria before its descent to collective suicide. The countries that are enduring a refugee crisis had no responsibility for creating it. Generating refugees is largely a responsibility of the rich and powerful, who now groan under the burden of a trickle of miserable victims whom they can easily accommodate.

The US-UK invasion of Iraq alone displaced some 4 million people, of whom almost half fled to neighbouring countries. And Iraqis continue to flee from a country that is one of the most miserable on earth after a decade of murderous sanctions followed by the sledgehammer blows of the rich and powerful that devastated the ruined country and also ignited a sectarian conflict that is now tearing the country and the region to shreds.

There is no need to review the European role in Africa, the

source of more refugees, now passing through the funnel created by the French-British-US bombing of Libya, which virtually destroyed the country and left it in the hands of warring militias. Or to review the US record in Central America, leaving horror chambers from which people are fleeing in terror and misery, joined now by Mexican victims of the trade pact which, predictably, destroyed Mexican agriculture, unable to compete with highly subsidised US agribusiness conglomerates.

The reaction of the rich and powerful United States is to pressure Mexico to keep US victims far from its own borders, and to drive them back mercilessly if they manage to evade the controls. The reaction of the rich and powerful European Union is to bribe and pressure Turkey to keep pathetic survivors from its borders and to herd those who escape into brutal camps.

Among citizens, there are honourable exceptions. But the reaction of the States is a moral disgrace, even putting aside their considerable responsibility for the circumstances that have compelled people to flee for their lives.

The shame is not new. Let us keep just to the United States, the most privileged and powerful country in the world, with incomparable advantages. Throughout most of its history it welcomed European refugees, to settle the lands taken by violence from the assassinated nations that dwelled in them. That changed with the Immigration Act of 1924, aimed at excluding particularly Italians and Jews. There is no need to dwell on their fate. Even after the war, survivors still confined to concentration camps were barred entry. Today, Roma are being expelled from France to horrible conditions in Eastern Europe, descendants of Holocaust victims, if anyone cares.

The shame is deep and persistent. The time has surely come to put it to an end and to try to attain some decent level of civilisation.

Acknowledgements

This book would not have been possible without the support of more than five hundred individual subscribers. I am deeply grateful for the brilliance, patience and generosity of the contributing authors, many of whom waived their contributor fee so that we could maximise the funds raised for the good causes. Many other people contributed significantly to making the book happen: Tameem Antoniades, Anthony Arnove, Cristina Bacchilega, Claire Conville, Allison DeFrees, Suzanne Fairless-Aitken, Tim Finch, Chris Gribble, David Grossman, Claudia Hammond, Antonia Karaisi, Grace Keane, Shyam Kumar, James Macdonald Lockhart, Dominic Matthews, Claire Malcolm, Elizabeth Meins, Florence Reynolds, Debbie Riby, Mary Robson, Sam Ruddock, Rose Simkins, Jo Thompson and Rebecca Wilkie. The funding campaign was assisted by events held at the Durham Book Festival and the Norwich and Norfolk Festival. I am grateful to our patron, Ninja Theory, for their especially generous support. This is my second book with Unbound, and it has once again been a delight to work with their incredible team. Special thanks to Mark Bowsher, Ella Chappell, Phil Connor, Becca Day-Preston, Caitlin Harvey, Rachael Kerr, John Mitchinson, Georgia Odd, Joelle Owusu, Anna Simpson, Miranda Ward and Amy Winchester.

Author Biographies

Leila Aboulela grew up in Sudan and moved, in her mid-twenties, to Scotland. A Caine Prize winner, her novels are *The Kindness of Enemies*, *The Translator* (one of the *New York Times*' '100 Notable Books of the Year'), *Minaret* and *Lyrics Alley* (Fiction Winner of the Scottish Book Awards). Her work has been translated into fifteen languages. Leila's new collection of stories is *Elsewhere, Home*.

Gillian Allnutt was born in London but has lived more than half her life (in chosen exile) in North East England. She has enjoyed the privilege of publishing under her own name and has produced nine collections of poetry. The latest, *wake*, was published in 2018. She has taught creative writing for thirty-five years, working with many and various groups of people, including asylum seekers in North East England from 2009–2011.

Damian Barr is an award-winning writer and columnist. *Maggie & Me*, his memoir about coming of age and coming out in Thatcher's Britain, was a BBC Radio 4 *Book of the Week* and *Sunday Times* Memoir of the Year, winning the Paddy Power Political Books 'Satire' Award and Stonewall Writer of the Year. Damian writes columns for the *Big Issue* and *High Life* and often appears on BBC

Radio 4. He is creator and host of his own Literary Salon which premieres work from established and emerging writers. His debut novel, *You Will Be Safe Here*, is published in 2019. Damian Barr lives in Brighton. @Damian_Barr

Noam Chomsky was born in Philadelphia, Pennsylvania, on 7 December 1928. He studied linguistics, mathematics, and philosophy at the University of Pennsylvania. In 1955, he received his Ph.D. from the University of Pennsylvania. Chomsky is Institute Professor (emeritus) in the Department of Linguistics and Philosophy at the Massachusetts Institute of Technology and Laureate Professor of Linguistics and Agnese Nelms Haury Chair in the Program in Environment and Social Justice at the University of Arizona. His work is widely credited with having revolutionised the field of modern linguistics. Chomsky is the author of numerous best-selling political works, which have been translated into scores of countries worldwide. Among his most recent books are *Hegemony or Survival, Failed States, Who Rules the World?, Requiem for the American Dream,* and *What Kind of Creatures Are We?*

Rishi Dastidar's poetry has been published by the BBC, *Financial Times, New Scientist,* Tate Modern and London's Southbank Centre amongst many others. A fellow of The Complete Works, the Arts Council England funded programme for poets of colour, he is a consulting editor at *The Rialto* magazine, a member of the Malika's Poetry Kitchen collective and serves as chair of the London-based writer development organisation Spread the Word. His debut collection *Ticker-tape* is published in the UK by Nine Arches Press, a poem from which was included in *The Forward Book of Poetry 2018*.

Peter Ho Davies' books include *The Welsh Girl*, longlisted for the Man Booker Prize, and most recently *The Fortunes*, winner of the Anisfield-Wolf Award. One of *Granta*'s 'Best of Young British Novelists', he's also a recipient of the PEN/Macmillan and John Llewellyn Rhys awards. Born in Coventry to Welsh and Chinese parents, he now teaches at the University of Michigan.

Louise Doughty is the author of eight novels including the bestseller *Apple Tree Yard*. She has been nominated for the Costa Novel Award, the Orange Prize for Fiction and the *Sunday Times* EFG Short Story Award. Her work has been translated into thirty languages. Her new novel, *Platform Seven*, will be published by Faber & Faber in 2019.

Salena Godden is the author of poetry collections *Under The Pier* (Nasty Little Press) and *Fishing in the Aftermath: Poems 1994–2014* (Burning Eye), along with the literary childhood memoir *Springfield Road* (Unbound) and the essay 'Shade' published in the groundbreaking anthology *The Good Immigrant* (Unbound). Her live poetry album *LIVEwire* was released with indie spoken word label Nymphs and Thugs and was shortlisted for the Ted Hughes Award. In July 2018 *Pessimism is for Lightweights: 13 pieces of courage and resistance* was published by Rough Trade

Books. Her viral poem 'Pessimism is for Lightweights' is currently a public poetry art piece displayed at the Arnolfini Gallery, Harbourside, Bristol.

Colin Grant is an author, historian and Associate Fellow in the Centre for Caribbean Studies, University of Warwick. His books include *Negro with a Hat: The Rise and Fall of Marcus Garvey* and a memoir of growing up in a Caribbean family in 1970s Luton, *Bageye at the Wheel*, which was shortlisted for the PEN/Ackerley Prize, 2013. As a producer for the BBC, Grant wrote and directed a number of radio drama documentaries including *A Fountain of Tears: The Murder of Federico Garcia Lorca*. He also writes for the *Guardian*, *TLS*, *New York Review of Books* and *Granta*.

Sam Guglani is a doctor and writer. He is a consultant clinical oncologist in Cheltenham, specialising in the management of lung and brain tumours. He has master's degrees in ethics (Keele, 2009) and creative writing (Oxford, 2014). He is a published poet; his column 'The Notes' is published by the *Lancet*; and his novel *Histories* is published by riverrun (Quercus Books, 2017). He is director and curator of Medicine Unboxed, a project he founded in 2009 to engage health professionals and the public in conversation around medicine, illuminated through the arts.

Matt Haig is the author of the internationally bestselling memoir *Reasons to Stay Alive*, along with six novels, including the bestselling *How to Stop Time*, and several award-winning children's books. His work has been translated into thirty languages. His latest non-fiction book, *Notes on a Nervous Planet*, was published in July 2018.

Aamer Hussein was born in Karachi in 1955 and moved to London in 1970. A graduate of SOAS, he has lectured at the Universities of London and Southampton, and writes in both English and Urdu. Since his first book of stories, *Mirror to the Sun* (1993), he has published five collections of stories, most recently *Love and its Seasons* (2017), and two novels, *Another Gulmohar Tree* (2009) and *The Cloud Messenger* (2011). He divides his time between London and Pakistan.

Anjali Joseph was born in Bombay and grew up in Warwickshire. She read English at Trinity College, Cambridge, and has worked as a journalist, English teacher, secretary, French teacher, and trainee accountant – and latterly teaches creative writing at Oxford. Her first novel, *Saraswati Park*, won the Betty Trask and Desmond Elliot Prizes and the Vodafone Crossword Book Award for fiction. She is completing her fourth novel, provisionally titled *Keeping in Touch*, from which 'In the Dark' is an extract.

A. L. Kennedy is an author of fiction, non-fiction and drama for a variety of age groups. Her work has been translated into over twenty languages and she has won a range of awards in a number of countries including the Costa Prize, the Heinrich Heine Prize and Austrian State Prize for International Literature.

Joanne Limburg is a writer, poet and creative writing lecturer. Her books include the memoirs *The Woman Who Thought Too Much* and *Small Pieces*, the novel *A Want of Kindness* and the poetry collections *Femenismo, Paraphernalia* and *The Autistic Alice*. She lives in Cambridge with her husband and son.

Rachel Mann is a Church of England priest, writer and scholar. The author of five books, her memoir of growing up trans, *Dazzling Darkness*, was a bestseller. Between 2009 and 2017 she was resident poet at Manchester Cathedral, and is currently Visiting Fellow at the Manchester Writing School, Manchester Metropolitan University. She holds a PhD on Victorian poetry and the Bible, and contributes to *Pause for Thought* on BBC Radio 2. When not writing on gender, sexuality and faith, she writes for the music press on prog, metal and folk music.

Tiffany Murray has been a Hay Festival fiction fellow, a Fulbright scholar and Senior Lecturer. Her novels *Diamond Star Halo* and *Happy Accidents* were shortlisted for the Bollinger Everyman Wodehouse Prize. Her latest novel is *Sugar Hall*.

Sara Nović is the author of the novel *Girl at War* (Random House, Little, Brown UK, 2015), which won the American Library Association Alex Award, was an *LA Times* book prize finalist, and was longlisted for the Baileys Women's Prize for Fiction. Her short fiction and essays have appeared in the *New York Times*, the *Guardian*, *Harper's*, *BOMB*, *Guernica*, *Electric Literature*,

TriQuarterly and others. Nović studied fiction and literary translation in the MFA at Columbia University. She is an assistant professor of creative writing at Stockton University, and the fiction editor for *Blunderbuss Magazine*.

Edward Platt is a writer and journalist. He is the author of *Leadville: A Biography of the A40,* which won a Somerset Maugham Award and the John Llewellyn Rhys Prize and was shortlisted for two other awards, and *The City of Abraham*. His new book, *The Great Flood,* will be published by Picador in 2019. He is a Contributing Writer at the *New Statesman* and a regular contributor to other newspapers and magazines.

Alex Preston is a prize-winning novelist and journalist. He teaches creative writing at the University of Kent. He has swum the Hellespont.

Tom Shakespeare is a sociologist and ethicist specialising in disability research. He was formerly at the World Health Organization, where he was a co-author of the *World Report on Disability* (2011). His books include *Disability Rights and Wrongs* and *Disability: The Basics*. Ten years ago, he wrote and performed a one-person show, *No Small Inheritance*, from which this chapter is adapted. Since then, his restricted growth (dwarfism) has led to spinal cord injury, so that he now mainly uses a wheelchair. He broadcasts regularly on BBC Radio 4.

Kamila Shamsie is the author of seven novels, which have been translated into over twenty languages. *Home Fire* won the Women's Prize for Fiction, was shortlisted for the Costa Novel Award and longlisted for the Man Booker Prize; *Burnt Shadows* was shortlisted for the Orange Prize for Fiction; and *A God in Every Stone* was shortlisted for the Baileys Women's Prize for Fiction. Three of her other novels (*In the City by the Sea, Kartography, Broken Verses*) have received awards from the Pakistan Academy of Letters. A Fellow of the Royal Society of Literature, and one of Granta's 'Best of Young British Novelists', she grew up in Karachi, and now lives in London.

Will Storr is an award-winning journalist and novelist. His work has appeared in titles such as the *Guardian Weekend, The Sunday Times Magazine* and *Esquire*. He is the author of four critically acclaimed books and teaches popular journalism and storytelling classes in London, at Guardian Masterclasses and the Faber Academy.

Preti Taneja was born and grew up in the UK. She has worked with UK youth charities and on minority and cultural rights in conflict and post-conflict zones. She teaches writing and human rights in prisons and universities. She is the co-founder of ERA Films, and of *Visual Verse*, the online anthology of art and words. Her debut novel *We That Are Young* (Galley Beggar Press) won the Desmond Elliott Prize 2018.

Marina Warner is a writer of fiction, cultural history and criticism. She has published award-winning studies of the cult of the Virgin

Mary (*Alone of All Her Sex*) and, recently, of the *Arabian Nights*, *Stranger Magic* (2011) and fairy tales (*From the Beast to the Blonde* and *A Very Short Introduction to Fairy Tale*). In 2015, she was awarded the Holberg Prize in the Arts and Humanities and was made DBE. She is Professor of English and Creative Writing at Birkbeck College, President of the Royal Society of Literature, and an Honorary Fellow of the Royal Academy. She is writing a book about sanctuary.

Endnotes

We Are the Champions, Salena Godden

[1] Jo uses the term autistic or autistic spectrum to broadly mean her condition of special needs. Since I began writing this, thanks to editor Charles Fernyhough, I've discovered that Williams Syndrome is seen as distinct from the autism spectrum, that they are different conditions that have different strengths and disabilities associated with them. I am grateful too to Professor Debbie Riby for sharing information about Williams Syndrome.

The Other Side of Gender, Rachel Mann

[1] 'Cisgender', as a gender theory term, has its origin in the Latin-derived prefix *cis,* meaning 'to the near side'. In this case, 'cis' refers to the alignment of gender identity with assigned gender at birth.

[2] 'Cis-het' is a contraction of the terms 'cisgender' and 'heterosexual'. In short, a 'cis-het' person is a straight person who is comfortable with the gender they were assigned at birth.

Living in a Country of Words: The Shelter of Stories, Marina Warner

[1] A record of each workshop can be found at storiesintransit.org. A report by Marina Warner on the two first workshops in 2016,

one in Oxford and one in Palermo, was published in the *Marvels &*
Tales journal under the title of 'Report: Bearer-Beings and Stories
in Transit/Storie in Transito': digitalcommons.wayne.edu/marvels/
vol31/iss1/9/. A section of the present essay is adapted from that
piece.

[2] See Mahmoud Darwish's poem 'We Travel Like Other People', in
Mahmoud Darwish, *Unfortunately, It Was Paradise: Selected Poems,*
trans. by Munir Akash and Carolyn Forché et al., University of
California Press, Berkeley, CA, 2013, p. 11.

[3] According to Jérémy Lachal, the director of Bibliothèques Sans
Frontières, the average time spent in a camp is seventeen years; see
librarieswithoutborders.org/4-years-of-the-ideas-box-1-million-
users-throughout-the-world/

[4] Personal communication, 4 August 2016.

[5] Alfred Korzybski, *Science and Sanity: An introduction to Non-
Aristotelian Systems and General Semantics,* Institute of General
Semantics, New York, NY,1995, p. 58.

[6] See Marina Warner, 'The Library in Fiction', in Alice Crawford
(ed.), *The Meaning of the Library: A Cultural History,* Princeton
University Press, Princeton, NJ, 2015, pp. 153–75.

[7] See 'Métaphore' in Abdelfattah Kilito, *Archéologies,* trans. by
Marina Warner and Clare Finburgh as 'Archaeology: Five Miniatures'
in *The White Review,* November 2013, thewhitereview.org/poetry/
archeology-five-miniatures/

[8] Seamus Heaney, Preface, *The Crane Bag Book of Irish Studies*
(1977–1981), eds. M. P. Hederman and R. Kearney, Blackwater
Press, Dublin, 1982.

[9] Terence Cave, *Thinking with Literature,* Oxford University Press, Oxford, 2016.

[10] Martin Kemp, "'Il Concetto dell'Anima" in Leonardo's Early Skull Studies', *Journal of the Warburg and Courtauld Institutes,* 34, 1971, pp. 115–34.

[11] Sallustius, *Concerning the Gods and the Universe, English and Ancient Greek,* ed. Arthur Darby Nock, Cambridge University Press, Cambridge, UK, [1926], 2013.

[12] See etsy.com/shop/Giocherenda#about

[13] Through the patient negotiations of Valentina Castagna with the Liceo Ferrara, one of the schools where some of the refugees are enrolled, and with the support of CPIA teachers such as Clelia Bartoli, the refugees/*minorenni* were given permission not to be at school on Thursday and Friday and to come and join Stories in Transit instead. The schools involved are CPIA Palermo 1, and Scuola Superiore F. Ferrara; CPIA is a school now chiefly attended by refugees who are unaccompanied minors, but it is originally an institution for drop-outs and includes Italian students (and some second generation migrants), including some girls. Several teachers came throughout: Nilla Palmeri, Leda Parisi, Lucia Barbera, Nicoletta Campisi, Rosalia Lando, Letizia Gullo and one male teacher, Gianfranco Coppola. We were also helped throughout by Valentina's very hard-working team – Maria Vaccaro and Alessandra Impagnatiello.

We spent Thursday to Saturday 16–18 November inclusive at the Associazione Santa Chiara, preparing for the event to be held on Sunday 19.

Unbound is the world's first crowdfunding publisher, established in 2011.

We believe that wonderful things can happen when you clear a path for people who share a passion. That's why we've built a platform that brings together readers and authors to crowdfund books they believe in – and give fresh ideas that don't fit the traditional mould the chance they deserve.

This book is in your hands because readers made it possible. Everyone who pledged their support is listed below. Join them by visiting unbound.com and supporting a book today.

David Aaron
Sarah Abanamy
Rebecca Abrams
Rick Adams
Caspar Addyman
Jamilah Ahmed
Sarah Ahmed
Hugh Aldersey-Williams
Ben Alderson-Day
Andre Aleman
Paul Allen
Richard Allen
Lulu Allison
Adam Alter
Emma Anderson
Tameem Antoniades

Sandra Armor
Ken Arnold
Jill Ashby
Richard Ashcroft
Joanna Atkinson-Hearn
David Baillie
Aidan Baker
Sarah Bakewell
Natalie Banner
David Barker
Nick Barley
Damian Barr
Elizabeth Barry
Stuart Bartholomew
Subat Bashir
Rachael Beale

Michael Bearpark
Sarah Beck
Emily Bell
Kathleen Bell
Vaughan Bell
Richard Bentall
Marco Bernini
Isabel Berwick
Dorothy Bishop
Anthony Blackmore
Charlie Blease
Otis Blease
Margaret Bluman
Becky Bolton
Anja Bolz
Andrew Booker
Rachel Booth
Lucy Bowes
Deborah Bowman
Jeanette Boyd
Alison Brabban
Tania Branigan
Jane Branney
Richard W H Bray
Georgina Brett
Alan Brice
Emma Bridger
Emily Britt
Jon Brock
Helen Brocklebank
Matthew Broome
Alistair Brown
Karl Brown

Gareth Buchaillard-Davies
Deb Budding
Andrea Burden
Nicholas Burton
Isabelle Butcher
Marcus Butcher
Mike Butcher
Annone Butler
Darren Butler
Emily Butterworth
Lisa Byford
Felicity Callard
Charlie Campbell
Susie Campbell
Edward Carey
Katy Carr
Mike Carver
Tom Cassels
Matteo Cella
Luna Centifanti
Tom Chatfield
Jen Chesters
Peter Chilvers
Antonia Chitty
Vera Chok
Thomas Christodoulides
Alex Clark
Geraldine Clarkson
Mary Coaten
Natalie Coe
Helene Collon
Jane Commane
Dr Suzanne Conboy-Hill

Juliet Conlin
Annabel Connor
Clare Connor
Lucy Connor
Stephen Connor
Wendy Constance
Martin Conway
Kevin Conyers
Christopher Cook
James Cook
Jill Cook
Jude Cook
Anne Cooke
David Cooper
Phil Corlett
Dirk Corstens
Lauren Couch
Robyn Cowan
Steve Crabtree
David Craig
Tom Craig
Chris Creegan
Richard Cripps
Kate Cross
John Cryan
Ann D'Mello
Melissa Dahl
Tim Dalgleish
Gillian Darley
Jane Darroch Riley
Rishi Dastidar
Graham Davey
Sara Davies

Paige Davis
Olivia Dawson
Sarah Day
Rachael de Moravia
Lee de Wit
Felicity Deamer
Geraldine Deas
Zsófia Demjén
Fiona Dewar
Michael Dickel
Sheila Dillon
Sarah Dilnot
Isobel Dixon
Sophie Dixon
Thomas Dixon
David Dobbs
Guy Dodgson
Kevin Donnellon
Kirsty Doole
Louise Doughty
Jane Draycott
Jo Drugan
Ever Dundas
Sophie Duport
David Dupuis
Christine and Tony Dyer
Carlie Edge
David Edmonds
Kathryn Edwards
Tuomas Eerola
Fiona Ellis
James Ellis
Camilla Elworthy

Daniel Endicott
Christopher English
Stefanie Enriquez-Geppert
Ilana Estreich
Max Farrar
Athena Fernyhough
Isaac Fernyhough
Justine Fieth
Nathan Filer
Tim Finch
John Findlay
Sarah Fishburn
Sarah Fisher
Des Fitzgerald
Steve Fleming
James Flint
Judith Ford
Sheila Ford
Imogen Forster
Paul Forster
William Foster
Ellie Fothergill
John Foxwell
G Francis
Keith Frankish
Daniel Freeman
Chris French
Uta Frith
David Fuller
Jana Funke
Hilary Gallo
Peter Garratt
Jane Garrison

Garvey's Ghost
Lynda GB
Tim Gee
Phil George
Clare Gibson
Sam Gilbert
Jodie Ginsberg
Jessica Gioia
Bruno Girin
Salena Godden
Silke Goebel
Miranda Gold
Sarah Goldser
Sophie Goldsworthy
James Good
Usha Goswami
Anita Goveas
Neil Gower
Alexander Graham
Huw Green
Linda Green
James Gregory-Monk
Kate Griffin
Rhett Griffiths
Bas Groes
Viv Groskop
Nancy Groves
Sacha Guglani
Roland Gulliver
Emine Gurbuz
Daniel Hahn
Sue Haldemann
Diana Hall

Kim Halsey
Lindsay Hamilton
Kate Hammer
Claudia Hammond
Sarah Hanson
Donna Hardcastle
Amy Hardy
Phoebe Harkins
Louise Harnby
Charles Harris
Cassian Harrison
Mick Harrison
Raisa Hassan
Rhodri Hayward
Kellyanne Healey
Iona Heath
Rachel Heath
David Hebblethwaite
Barbara Henderson
David Hendy
Diana Henry
Philip Hewitt
Rachel Hewitt
E O Higgins
Jonathan Hoare
Jessica Hobson
Ted Hodgkinson
Lois Holzman
Helen Hood
Joe Hopper
Aidan Horner
Morgan G. Hough
Marie Hrynczak

Kenneth Hugdahl
Robin Humphrey
Russ Hurlburt
Umer Hussain
Shona Illingworth
Robin Ince
Amy Izycky
Patricia Jackson
Simon James
Simon J. James
Harriet Jane
Åsa Jansson
Renaud Jardri
Julia Jary
Simon Jary
Neil Jasani
Sian Jay
Christian Jeffery
Alok Jha
Arlene Johnstone
Alice Jolly
Mike Jones
Frances Keeton
Tina Keil
Sophie Kelly
James Kennaway
Paul Kent
Rachael Kerr
Dan Kieran
Jill Kieran
Lindsay King
Peter J. King
David Kleinman

Joel Krueger
Roman Krznaric
Maneesh Kuruvilla
Josh Lacey
Paul Laity
Ed Lake
Line Langebek
Fiona Larkin
Fionnuala Larkin
Frank Larøi
Ewan Lawrie
Hilary Leevers
Jenny Lewis
Jane Lidstone
Joanne Limburg
Catherine Lloyd
Hélène Loevenbruck
Eleanor Longden
Catherine Loveday
Christina Luest
Tanya Luhrmann
Raphael Lyne
José Machado
Jane Macnaughton
Laurie Maguire
Patrick Makin
Claire Malcolm
Jane Manley
Ita Marquess
Mandy Marsden
Dean Marshall
James Marsters
Caroline Martin

Harriet Martin
Paula Martin
Margaret Masson
François Matarasso
Clare Matterson
Jacqueline Maurice
Victoria McArthur
Nora McClelland
Teresa McCormack
Una McCormack
Linda McGowan
Robert Mclean
Tom McLeish
Catherine McMahon
Bairbre Meade
Luke Mendham
Jane Middlemiss
Philip Middleton
Rachel Middleton
Kiran Millwood Hargrave
Margo Milne
Kevin Mitchell
John Mitchinson
Gemma Modinos
Anibal Monasterio Astobiza
Chris Moore
Frank Moore
James Moore
Andrew Morris
Blake Morrison
Catriona Morrison
Tara Morse
Helen Mort

Peter Moseley
Melissa Mostyn
Graham Murray
Tiffany Murray
David Napthine
Deborah Nash
Carlo Navato
Joanne Neely
Antony Nelson
Gary Nicol
Katharine Norbury
Mike O'Brien
Joseph O'Dea
Eleanor O'Keeffe
MaryClare O'Brien
Silvia Orr
Angelica Ortiz de Gortari
Marilyn Over
Femi Oyebode
Scott Pack
Mike Page
Cath Palgrave
Sarah Passingham
Jaimie Pattison
Victoria Patton
Hannah Pawlby
Susan Pawlby
Jonathan Peelle
Richard Pemberton
Hugo Perks
Elizabeth Perry
Johann Perry
Sarah Perry

Emmanuelle Peters
James Peto
Elizabeth Pillar
Kate Plaisted-Grant
Edward Platt
Giulia Poerio
Justin Pollard
Gurleen Popli
Max Porter
Adam Powell
Hilary Powell
Chris Power
Alex Preston
Rebecca Priestley
Mel Pryor
Marleen Raaijmakers
Matthew Railton
Gita Ralleigh
Jonathan Ratty
Alison Reed
Nic Regan
Michael Regnier
Ella Rhodes
Sarah Rhydderch
Ruth Ricker
Imogen Robertson
Lucia Robertson Glass
Rachael Robinson
David Robson
Mary Robson
Richard Roche
Lisa Rodan
Andreas Roepstorff

William Rood
Arthur Rose
Nancy M Ruff
Caitlin Russell
James Russell
Ian Sample
@samschulzstudio
Sarah Sandow
Lisa Sargood
Corinne Saunders
Nicky Sawicki
Tim Saxton
Anna Sayburn Lane
Juliet Schofield
Ann Searight Christiano
Fred Searle
Rebecca Searle
Elena Semino
Anil Seth
Farhana Shaikh
Tom Shakespeare
Tracy Shaw
Valentina Short
Pam Shurmer-Smith
Daniela Sieff
Rose Simkins
Jon Simons
Carole Simpson
Dan Smith
Marc Smith
MTA Smith
Nigel Smith
Prof Barry C Smith

Janet Smyth
Richard Smyth
Sonia Friedman Productions
Heather Speight
Hugo Spiers
Mark Spivey
Connie St Louis
Tom Stafford
Martin Stals
Rosie Stanbury
Nicola Stewart
Kathleen Stock
Rebecca and Andrew Stoeckle
Harriet Stott
Lauren Strickland
Kate Summers
Jon Sutton
Peter Sutton
Kate Swindlehurst
Alicja Syska
Frank Tallis
Barbara Taylor
Valentina Terrinoni
Teobesta Tesfa Endrias
Lore Thaler
Bill Thompson
Elspeth Thomson
Katie Thornburrow
Georgie Thurlby
Irmgard Tischner CritPsy
Charles Tongue
Kirty Topiwala
Susannah Tresilian

Manos Tsakiris
Tina Tse
Voula Tsoflias
Michelle Turner
Jon Turney
Wendy Tuxworth
Imogen Tyler
Eva Ullrich
Rachel Upthegrove
Anna Vaught
Mark Vent
Andrew Vidgen
Gaia Vince
William Viney
David Vogelsang
Judi Walsh
Miranda Ward
Thomas Ward
Flavie Waters
Tiffany Watt Smith
Patricia Waugh
Martin Webb
Valerie Webb

Venetia Welby
Katrina Whalley
Margaret White
Simon White
Sam Wilkinson
Elizabeth Williams
Ian Williams
John Williams
Elizabeth Winter
Devra Wiseman
Angela Woods
Robert Woodshaw
Laura Wright
Martin Wroe
Hazal Elif Yalvaç
Sophie Yauner
Rachel Yorke
Ashleigh Young
Amanda M. Young-Hauser
Hellen Jing Yuan
Leah Zakss
Anna Zammit